Meeting the Costs of Health Care:

THE BAY AREA EXPERIENCE AND THE NATIONAL ISSUES

By MARGARET GREENFIELD

1972

INSTITUTE OF GOVERNMENTAL STUDIES

University of California, Berkeley

Library of Congress Cataloging in Publication Data

Greenfield, Margaret.
Meeting the costs of health care.

1. Insurance, Health--San Francisco Bay region.
2. Insurance, Health--United States. I. California.
University. Institute of Governmental Studies.
II. Title.
HD7102.U4G718 368.4'2'00973 72-5657
ISBN 0-87772-086-X

$4.50

Meeting the Costs of Health Care:

The Bay Area Experience and the National Issues

Contents

Foreword

The quality of life enjoyed by many residents of the United States is severely impaired by deficiencies in the medical service and health care they receive. This is true despite the existence of excellent hospitals, large numbers of first-rate doctors, unexcelled medical research facilities, and a huge pharmaceutical establishment busily turning out new drugs.

But all is not well with health care, because people are not getting the help they need on a regular, comprehensive and continuing basis. The causes are many: medical, economic, organizational, fiscal. Instead of a compassionate service rendered to mankind, medicine and health care are too often treated as marketable commodities, huckstered to those who can afford to buy, but withheld from those who cannot pay. Doctors are scarce in rural areas and small towns. Even in the metropolis, poor people and racial and ethnic minorities receive inadequate care, and their health records show reduced longevity, higher infant mortality, and greater incidence of disease and chronic ailments than other groups experience. Moreover, few households have adequate protection against the catastrophic illnesses that can undermine a thriving family's economic position.

Medical care also suffers from other handicaps, in addition to maldistribution of resources and inadequate spreading of risk. There is a basic shortage of personnel, exacerbated by the fact that medical practice and hospital administration are heavily bureaucratized fields of endeavor. For cheaper and more expeditious service, greater flexibility is needed in the use of manpower. Increased freedom in deploying human resources can facilitate judicious arrangements placing greater reliance on nurses, paramedical personnel and other supportive staff, who can be trained in aspects of health care, but who need not hold M.D. degrees. Because there is also a scarcity of good general-purpose physicians, the output of doctors who are willing and able to engage in general practice should be stepped up. Of all the causes of medical service and health care deficiencies, however, probably the biggest source of trouble is the failure either to control costs or to distribute them on an equitable basis.

The problem is clearly not a matter of national inability to afford first-rate service. Ironically, the world's wealthiest country is also the only modern industrial power without a national health service for all its people. Instead, we are now in an "in-between" stage, financing health care through a multitude of private, group, semipublic and public systems.

These complicated arrangements are obviously far from perfect, but they are what we have for the time being, and we are well advised to understand their workings. What is more, future systems of medical service will emerge from present health care organization and practice, and be based in part on what we have learned from it.

At first glance, the uninitiated reader must find the complexity of health care administration and finance scarcely comprehensible. Accordingly it is evident that Margaret Greenfield has performed a signal service in organizing and making sense of a wealth of material on health care in the San Francisco Bay Area. Her long acquaintance with and expertise in the field of social legislation have uniquely qualified her for the demanding task. Further, her study of financing health care in one of the most medically sophisticated of the nation's metropolitan regions also helps establish guidelines for understanding both the solid accomplishments achieved (which are substantial), and the remaining deficiencies (which may be even greater).

Although focussed primarily on the Bay Area, this monograph closes with an examination of national policy issues posed by the health care crisis. Severe and continued inadequacies, plus surging costs experienced as we fumble, tinker and patch, are pushing the United States almost inevitably toward comprehensive national financing, as well as toward new forms of health care delivery. The experience of the San Francisco Bay Area will almost certainly play a significant role in determining what the new systems of the future look like and how well they work.

Stanley Scott
Assistant Director

Preface

Both public and private health care expenditures are at an all-time high. National expenditures for personal health care in the fiscal year 1969-70 amounted to $58 billion. This was 60 percent higher than in fiscal 1965-66, the year before Medicare began, and almost 12 percent higher than in fiscal 1968-69.[1] More than half the increase was produced by the rise in prices. Expenditures for personal health care exclude medical facilities construction, medical research, public health activities, administrative expenses of public programs and the net cost of insurance.

Medical care prices have shot ahead twice as fast as the general price level. It was in July 1965 that Congress amended the Social Security Act to provide health insurance for the aged: Medicare. From 1965 through 1969, the cost of medical care rose 27 percent while all other items in the Bureau of Labor Statistics consumer price index rose only 16 percent.[2] In that period physicians' fees rose 28 percent, according to the index, and hospital daily service charges rose 67 percent.*

---

*Preliminary figures for 1970 indicate a slowdown in rising cost of medical care services compared to the general price level. The consumer price index for all items, less medical care, rose 4.9 percent over 1969, while cost of medical care services rose 5.2 percent. The index for physicians' fees was 6.2 percent higher and for hospital daily service charges 10.1 percent higher.

Hospital costs have zoomed higher than any other item. In the last 20 years, they increased 386 percent while prices generally went up only 58 percent.

Premiums for every type of health insurance have followed suit. Since 1965 rates for private insurance of all types have increased, while rates for medical insurance under Medicare accelerated 77 percent from July 1, 1966 to July 1, 1970.* Net cost of prepayment--the difference between private health insurance premium charges and benefit expenditures--climbed 25 percent between 1965 and 1969.[3]

Talk of a national health insurance program is rife. Headlines in the daily press accent public concern:

> "Zooming Costs Bring Call for National Health Insurance"
>
> "Governors Urge National Health Insurance"
>
> "Senate Bill--Health Care for Everyone"
>
> "Citizen's Plan--Compulsory Health Insurance for All"
>
> "Two Doctor Groups Back National Health Insurance Plan"
>
> "Meany Vows to Press for National Health Care"

A wide range of national health plans is being suggested. Types of plans and timing are moot. What does the future hold for protection against the sometimes catastrophic cost of illness? To what extent are Bay Area residents protected now?

It was known through other studies that as of December 31, 1967 insurance against the cost of hospital care was held by 81 percent of the California population

---

*As of July 1, 1971, another increase in premium rates for medical insurance under Medicare results in a cumulative rise of 87 percent since 1966.

under age 65; protection against surgical costs, by 75 percent; and insurance for regular medical expense, by 67 percent.[4] Further, the California Department of Industrial Relations estimated that in 1968, 97 percent of unionized workers in California, 97 percent in the San Francisco-Oakland area and 99 percent in the San Jose area were covered by negotiated health insurance.[5]

How does this insurance work? Who underwrites it? Who pays for it? What are the benefits? What are the limitations?

METHODOLOGY OF THE SURVEY

To obtain some answers to these questions, in 1969 and early 1970 arrangements were explored in the nine Bay Area counties--Alameda, Contra Costa, Marin, Napa, San Francisco, San Mateo, Santa Clara, Solano and Sonoma. Information on employer-employee health care plans was solicited from both large and small industrial employers, from collectively bargained health and welfare trust funds, and from federal, state and local governmental employers.

Organizations Included

A questionnaire was sent to every employer of 100 or more persons listed in the California Manufacturers' Association *1968 Register*, and to a 20 percent sample of smaller employers in the area. Schedules were also sent to leading financial and public utilities firms, from a list furnished by the California State Chamber of Commerce. In all, 923 questionnaires were sent to this group. By the time analysis began, however, a total of 81 of the establishments queried had ceased to function in the Bay Area, leaving a working universe of 842 industrial establishments.

Since many of the respondents limited their replies to salaried employees, stating they had no information on hourly workers, 11 labor union plans were also examined through the courtesy of officials of union-management health and welfare trust funds.

In addition, the questionnaire, suitably modified, went to personnel officers of the nine county governments and to 65 cities with populations over 5000. A similar schedule was sent to 159 school districts whose average daily attendance ranged from 300 to 110,000. In order to round out the picture, another aspect of the health care services was included: governmental provision for other population groups--veterans, the aged, the poor.

Personal interviews provided specific information on both Bay Area community health centers and county provision for medical care of needy persons not eligible for any of the state or state-federal programs. Sources of information on other programs will be found in the notes.

Limitations of Survey Data

The schedule asked for much detailed data on the health plans covering a majority of employees in the establishment.* Complete response would have required considerable effort by the respondent, a circumstance that probably discouraged extensive participation. Nevertheless, three out of five questionnaires (58.6 percent) sent to the industrial and financial firms were completed and returned. However, not all questions were answered by all respondents. The return from firms with 100 or more employees amounted to 66 percent, and that from the smaller firms to 47 percent. Responding firms employed approximately 300,000 persons in 1969, about a third of all persons employed in this sector of the Bay Area economy.

---

*See Appendix for copy of schedule.

Replies were received from 100 percent of the counties and 85 percent of the cities, but only 54 percent of the school districts replied. Information was therefore supplemented by material from a survey made by the California Teachers Association.[6]

It must be emphasized that many types of employers were not reached, and that workers in construction, transportation, trade, amusement and recreation, for example, were not included by the questionnaire. (Plans covering many of these workers are described in the collectively bargained programs.) Moreover, medical care plans of fraternal societies, private schools and colleges were not examined nor were medical plans covering students at either public or private colleges. Limited funds prevented such an encyclopaedic survey.

The reader is cautioned therefore that the data based on questionnaires should not be extrapolated. They must be looked upon as general indicators rather than a precise reflection of insurance coverage for all Bay Area residents. Despite these limitations, the study illustrates clearly the present patchwork of programs that however inadequately, help the American public to pay its medical bills.

Thanks and Ever Thanks

Without the help of the 650 respondents to the questionnaire and that of the health and welfare trust fund officials who made supplementary information available, this study could not have been completed. The author is deeply grateful to each, including those who took the trouble to say they had no health plan or that they were no longer in business.

Also gratefully acknowledged are the suggestions made by the late Mark M. Berke, by Henrik L. Blum, Alfred W. Childs, Robert Jackson, Harriet Nathan, Alberta W. Parker, Bruce Payer, Jerome L. Schwartz and Don Vial who read the first draft. Many thanks are also due to

Hazel B. Karns and her staff including Katherine Castro who typed the manuscript, for their contribution in preparing the book for publication.

WHAT FOLLOWS

The first chapter describes various types of health insurance in general and gives a brief account of their development. The health care plans reported by respondents from commercial firms in the Bay Area are analyzed in Chapter II, as are selected collectively bargained health and welfare trust funds. Health care plans for governmental employees and publicly sponsored programs for special population groups, including aged persons, military personnel, veterans and medically needy persons, are summarized in Chapters III and IV. Finally, differing views of public policy regarding delivery of health care services are discussed in Chapter V.

February 1971

CHAPTER *I*

Insurance Against the Costs of Medical Care

Nearly two-thirds (65 percent) of the total expenditures for personal health care in the fiscal year 1969-70 was paid by the private sector of the economy, the sector with which this monograph is immediately concerned. Not to be overlooked, however, is the great rise in governmental expenditures for such care: from 22 percent of the total in the fiscal year 1966 to 35 percent in fiscal 1970. This shift in source of funding is almost entirely attributable to the advent of Medicare, the federal program of health insurance for the aged.[1]

For most American families, a substantial part of their medical bills must be paid out of income and resources--or loans--and the rest through some type of insurance. The proportion of private funds paid directly by individuals and families has been declining, from 68 percent in 1949-50 to 40 percent in 1969-70.[2] Consumers pay out-of-pocket costs for uninsured hospital charges, for most physicians' office or home services, and for almost all other out-of-hospital services.

The substantial reduction in the proportion of medical costs that the individual must bear directly has come about through a wide variety of programs that range from individual purchase of commercial indemnity insurance against the costs of illness to industry-wide programs of comprehensive group health care fully paid by the employer. Private insurance met 24 percent of all consumer personal health care expenses (not including the net cost of obtaining health insurance) in calendar 1969. In that year insurance covered 35 percent of hospital care expenses and 34 percent of expenditures for physician services, but only 4 percent of the costs for other types of care.[3]

Sixty percent of the persons enrolled in health care plans were covered by the commercial insurance companies in 1968, 36 percent by Blue Cross-Blue Shield and 4 percent by independent plans.[4]

STATEWIDE PUBLIC PROGRAMS

Although this study is directed principally toward private provision for paying the costs of medical care, two statewide California programs should be noted. These are programs that help working people meet hospital and medical bills: workmen's compensation and unemployment compensation disability insurance (UCD). Most voluntary insurance contracts specifically exclude injuries or illnesses whose treatment is covered by a governmental facility or is under workmen's compensation. That portion of hospital bills paid by UCD is usually deducted from reimbursement for hospitalization, although some collectively bargained contracts specify that benefits are paid in addition to UCD.

Workmen's Compensation

Workmen's compensation, the oldest major social insurance program in the nation, is designed to partially offset wage loss and to provide some reimbursement for medical costs incurred by persons injured while working. The cost of the program is borne by employers, usually through commercial insurers. The California law provides for compulsory participation for both private and public employers, although some employments are excepted from coverage. Among these are: servants who work for one employer less than 52 hours a week, most casual employees, volunteers working for nonprofit organizations, public clerks and deputies serving without remuneration. Occupational diseases are covered as well as job injuries, and medical benefits apply to both types of disability. Payment to those who provide service is set by a fee schedule.

Unemployment Compensation Disability Insurance

Persons covered by the California unemployment compensation law are also covered by disability insurance when ill, after a seven-day waiting period. The program compensates primarily for wage loss but also provides a token hospital expense benefit. An insured disabled person confined to a hospital by his doctor is entitled to an additional cash benefit of $12 a day up to 20 days in one disability period. There is no medical expense benefit. The program is financed by a one percent tax on the employee's wages up to $7400. The basic law has been in effect since 1946, and the hospital benefit was added in 1953. Farm workers who earn $300 or more in covered employments during the base year have been included since January 1964.* Nearly 1.3 million persons in the Bay Area are covered by the program.

DEVELOPMENT OF PRIVATE INSURANCE[5]

Insurance is a mechanism for spreading among many individuals the cost of personal risk to any of them. Americans have long been heavily insured against losses by death, fire, accident and various other risks. In recent years great strides have been made in health

---

*About 19,000 hired workers are employed in Bay Area agriculture. Approximately 65 percent would be eligible.

insurance through individual and group contracts.* With employers frequently paying part and sometimes all of the premiums, the economic hardships resulting from illness have been greatly reduced for a large segment of the population.

The extent of voluntary protection against the costs of illness for persons under age 65 in the U.S. attests to the acuity of the insurance industry and to public pressures as organized groups became more sophisticated about insurance contracts. This record was achieved principally through group plans connected with employment. Group coverage makes insurance available at the lowest possible cost, facilitates the payment of premiums through payroll deductions and allows some employees to qualify for insurance who would not be insurable under the rules of individual underwriting. Where the employer contributes to the cost of the premium, moreover, his payment is a business expense for income tax purposes. Similarly, the employee need not pay taxes on compensation received in the form of health and welfare benefits (instead of money).

The principal growth in group insurance against the costs of medical care occurred during and since World War II. The War Labor Board restrictions on wage increases during a period of labor shortages led to union-management agreements on the substitution of "fringe benefits" for higher wages. Today most large private employers and many smaller ones provide such insurance protection to their employees not only as a result of collective bargaining, but also by administrative decision.[6]

---

*The term "health insurance" is used throughout this monograph because it is the one commonly used. It might better be called "sickness insurance" since the aim of most programs is to pay for treatment and not for prevention.

The Impetus for Insurance

The impetus for voluntary health insurance came from the Depression era of the 1930s, when the health services were affected like every other field. In order to live, many doctors had to accept goods and services from patients without money, and to take part-time work with public health departments and even non-medical jobs when they could get them.

Hospitals were even harder hit. Their expenses continued while income from patients dwindled and private philanthropy dried up. These circumstances gave rise to the first of the prepaid group hospitalization plans, started by Baylor University Hospital in Texas. Seeking to stabilize its costs early in the Depression, the hospital offered a prepaid group hospitalization plan. For an annual fee of $6 per person, the hospital was willing to provide up to three weeks' care in semi-private rooms, including the services of its professional and nonprofessional staff. Public school teachers, bank employees, city firemen and policemen, graduate nurses and newspaper employees bought the plan in quick succession.

The next year, seven hospitals in the City of Sacramento in California set up an insurance company to sell a similar plan. A number of other cities also set up joint plans. These plans were approved "in principle" by the American Hospital Association, which later gave formal approval to plans that met official standards. Approved plans were permitted to use the Blue Cross symbol.

Before the Depression, some of the casualty insurance companies had sold accident and disability insurance, whose main purpose was to provide a weekly income to persons unable to work because of an accident or illness. Some policies included a small sum for hospital bills and others included an additional allowance toward payment of surgical bills. The greater part of these policies were written for individuals. During the Depression the insurance carriers lost heavily on these policies and wrote relatively few new ones before the late thirties, when they observed the success of the group hospitalization plans. In 1936 Blue Cross dominated the hospital insurance field, but by 1949 the indemnity insurance carriers had overtaken Blue Cross and have since continued to widen their influence.

The 1940s also saw the founding of plans set up by state medical societies to provide surgical, obstetrical, x-ray and anesthesia services in the hospital on a fixed fee basis for persons below a specified income level and on a cash indemnity basis for those above that level. Physician out-of-hospital benefits were added later, with California taking the lead. These plans are the mark of the Blue Shield organizations.

APPROACHES TO HEALTH CARE INSURANCE

A group health care plan provides for one or more of the following: (1) life insurance or death benefits; (2) accidental death and dismemberment benefits; (3) indemnity for income lost because of disability; and (4) benefits for hospital, surgical and regular medical expense. This monograph is confined to the last category: provision of benefits for hospital, surgical and medical expense.

Medical care benefits may be provided on either a cash indemnity or a service basis.* On an indemnity basis, the carrier specifies the extent of its financial liability for each item of care or for total care and makes cash reimbursement to the individual. When benefits are provided on a service basis, liability is expressed in terms of services to be provided without charge, and may specify charges for certain other services.

---

*It should be noted that most service plans now have indemnity features, and some indemnity plans have service features.

Health care plans are underwritten by commercial insurance companies, by voluntary organizations like Blue Cross and Blue Shield, by prepaid comprehensive group practice plans like Kaiser, or by individual practice prepayment plans sponsored by medical society foundations.

Health and welfare trust funds, set up by collective bargaining and usually jointly administered by management and labor, for the most part insure their members against the costs of illness through one or more of these arrangements. Some large employers are self-insured, and some are self-insured for one aspect of care and use commercial insurance for another. In 1966 there were 402 organizations in California that were writing health insurance.[7]

Both service plan and indemnity plan underwriters are willing to tailor an insurance policy to the needs and requirements of any given group, with regard to benefits and premiums. Package plans are also available for groups that do not prepare their own specifications. Desired benefits vary from group to group, and the amount of premium that can be paid often dictates the benefits to be included.

The commercial insurance companies' share of total premium income has been rising over the years, from 47 percent in 1950 to 54 percent in 1968, at the expense of the Blues and the independent plans. This gain was all in the field of group policies. They rose from 26 percent in 1950 to 40 percent in 1968, while individual policy premiums dropped from 21 to 14 percent.[8]

Commercial Carriers

Insurance against the costs of illness is underwritten by insurance companies in several ways. Some companies sell individual policies only, but most now sell both to individual applicants and to small as well as large groups. Group health insurance has become more available for small firms than it was formerly. For many years group insurance was limited by state laws to groups of 25 or more, but most states now limit the minimum to 10 or fewer for employer-employee groups. In the Bay Area, insurance is available for groups as small as five.[9]

Group insurance accounts for the major portion of the health insurance benefits in force with insurance companies. Shortly after commencing to write group hospital expense insurance, the indemnity companies began developing a policy providing protection against doctors' fees for surgical operations and obstetrical procedures. Two types of policies are available under commercial insurance: "basic" and "major medical."

Basic Policies

A basic benefit plan reimburses the individual by specified amounts for cost of medical service within the limits of coverage. Basic plans underwritten for group coverage are more flexible than policies written for individuals. Although the insurance carrier takes into account the age, sex, geographic location, employment and income status of employees eligible to participate, as well as possible occupational hazards, the policy is based on group averages and not individual characteristics. A group plan, moreover, does not ordinarily require individual evidence of insurability.

Major Medical Policies

Major medical insurance is designed to protect the individual against extraordinary medical expense. It usually, but not always, supplements a basic plan and pays for many expenses not included or exceeding the limits set in the basic plan. A broad range of out-of-hospital services as well as hospital care is covered. The individual participates in the cost of care by paying a specified initial sum, called a "deductible," and a percentage of all additional expenditures, called "copayment" or "coinsurance."*

The deductible must be paid within specific time intervals, usually a year. In a few plans it is applied to the period of disability. The deductible applies separately to individual family members as well as to the primary policyholder. In some policies the deductible is satisfied for the entire family if three deductibles have been paid within the year. Expenditures for health care services not covered by the policy are not counted toward satisfying the deductible (e.g., dental or optometric care).

Subject to the deductible and coinsurance amounts, major medical plans pay for all covered expenses up to a specified aggregate maximum. In most plans an individual can become eligible for a full new maximum after $1000 in benefits have been paid and evidence of insurability is submitted (i.e., good health). Many group plans provide for automatic reinstatement up to $1000 in benefits at the beginning of the calendar year without evidence of insurability.

THE NONPROFIT BLUES

Blue Cross and Blue Shield are nonprofit, voluntary health-care prepayment plans. Blue Cross is hospital controlled, and in the past covered only hospital

---

*In defense of the deductible clause and copayment, it is claimed that if the insured is made to share directly in the cost of the service he receives, he will be motivated to purchase care economically and will be less likely to use unneeded services. On the other hand, deductibles and copayment are said to impede people in lower income groups from seeking care as soon as they need it. Organized labor in the past has strongly disapproved of major medical policies on this ground.

services (excluding those of private physicians), generally on a service-benefit basis. Blue Shield, which is physician governed, paid only for the services of physicians (medical or surgical), at first only in the hospital and later in the doctor's office or the patient's home. Today contracts can be made with either Blue Cross or Blue Shield that provide both in-hospital and out-of-hospital benefits.* Contracts for major medical benefits are also written by both. There are sizable differences in coverage by plans in different parts of the country and sometimes within the same vicinity.

Blue Cross

In their basic contracts, Blue Cross plans generally offer service benefits rather than cash indemnities and are written both on an individual and a group basis. The subscriber's contract spells out the specific services to which he is entitled in any affiliated hospital, regardless of the hospital's charges. Payment for care is made by Blue Cross directly to the hospital rather than to the subscriber. Hospital coverage varies from 21 to 365 days, with most groups covered for 70 to 100 days.

Basic Blue Cross plans also offer surgical coverage, in-hospital physician visits, and also out-of-hospital benefits. Plans are frequently coordinated with Blue Shield plans and with supplementary or extended benefits (major medical).

Although most Blue Cross premiums were originally based on a "community rating," now each group over a given size is rated by experience. Blue Cross in northern California is administered through the Hospital

---

*In California the two plans compete with each other. In many states, however, the two work together and complement each other.

Service of California, founded in 1936 with the financial assistance of the Alameda County Medical Society.

Blue Shield

California Physicians Service (CPS), a Blue Shield agency, was established by the California Medical Association in 1939, largely as an answer to the threat of a state health insurance system then being advocated by Governor Culbert Olson and organized labor. CPS markets various programs based upon the service desired and the income level of the group or persons to be covered.

A participating physician may charge the difference between his usual fees and the Blue Shield fee schedule if the patient's income is greater than the income level designated by his health plan policy.* Nonparticipating physicians charge their usual and customary fees. In some cases, reimbursement by a Blue Shield program covers the physician's charges; in others the patient must make up the difference between his CPS fee coverage and the physician's charge.

Subscribers may select any licensed physician or surgeon.

MEDICAL SOCIETY FOUNDATIONS

A number of "Foundations for Medical Care," organized by the county medical societies, are found in northern California. Only two at present exist in the Bay Area: in Sonoma County and in Santa Clara County. Foundation plans contract with participating member physicians, with employers and labor unions, and with commercial insurance carriers or the Blues.

---

*Many CPS contracts today cover "usual and customary" fees, paying contracting physicians according to a variable system rather than a fee schedule.

Medical society foundations for medical care stipulate benefit standards and set fee schedules. Foundations review all claims from physicians and hospitals in the interest of cost and quality controls. Participating doctors practice on a solo fee-for-service basis but agree to accept the foundation's fee schedules as full payment. The actual underwriting and sale of policies is left to insurance companies that are willing to accept the foundation's standards and claims procedures.

Providers of service are paid through the foundation, and the insurance carrier then reimburses the foundation.

COMPREHENSIVE PREPAYMENT PLANS*

Comprehensive community health care plans offer a broad scope of medical services--preventive, diagnostic and curative--in the hospital and out of the hospital for a fixed monthly prepayment. These plans may be: (1) open panel, in which the professional personnel agree to accept stipulated fees but also have outside practices; or (2) closed panel, in which the professional personnel practice chiefly within the plan, and benefits are available to members only at plan facilities.

Comprehensive prepayment plans usually pay doctors and hospitals an agreed-upon amount for each member per

---

*Prepaid group practice is here described at length since it is advocated by many as a possible means of improving the delivery of health care services. Federal health planners foresee encouragement of comprehensive prepaid group practice in any national medical care program, because they believe that such practice is more economical, can control overusage and employ auxiliary medical personnel. President Nixon's 1971 health care proposals advocate this type of practice as "health management organizations."

month (capitation payment), rather than an amount for each service rendered (fee for service). Out-of-pocket costs for covered services are minimal for the primary person insured and, depending on the contract, for the family as well. Premium rates are usually based on the costs of serving the entire covered community (community rating). Employers and other participating groups generally offer their members a choice between the group practice prepayment plan and an indemnity or service-benefit plan.

Kaiser Foundation Health Plan is the largest such plan in the country, with most of its members at present in California, but with a substantial number also in Denver, Portland, Cleveland and Hawaii. Another well-known California group plan is the Ross-Loos Medical Group, Los Angeles, in operation since 1929.

Outside the state, prominent plans are the Health Insurance Plan of Greater New York (HIP); Community Health Association, Detroit, Michigan (CHA); Group Health Association of Washington, D.C. (GHA); Group Health Cooperative of Puget Sound, Seattle, Washington (GHC). The last two are organized as consumer cooperatives.

Some plans include hospital service in the prepayment fee. Of those listed above, hospitalization is provided by the Kaiser plan, GHA, GHC and CHA. Ross-Loos covers hospitalization through an affiliated insurance company, and HIP requires members to subscribe to Blue Cross or some other hospital insurance plan. Kaiser, CHA and GHA have their own hospital facilities, and the others use community hospitals.

Boards of directors vary in the different plans. Business and industrial leaders comprise the Kaiser boards.* HIP and CHA boards represent community leaders.

---

*Organized labor in California has long sought a voice in the Kaiser health plan direction.

GHA and GHC boards are elected by consumer-members of the two cooperatives. Ross-Loos is governed by physician-owners.

Methods of compensating providers of services also differ. Kaiser and HIP contract with medical groups that are independent partnerships, paid on a capitation basis. CHA contracts with a hospital that employs the physicians, and payments are on a cost-reimbursement basis. GHA and GHC medical services are provided by an organized medical staff, paid on a cost-reimbursement basis. Ross-Loos is physician owned.

All the plans used community rating except Ross-Loos which experience-rates subscriber groups, i.e., on the basis of utilization experience.

Common Characteristics

Although the plans vary in these aspects, they have many characteristics in common:

1. Prepayment funds are used for staff and facilities to provide a broad range of medical services.
2. Physician services are provided in the doctor's office, in the home and in the hospital.
3. Care is not limited to illness or accidents. Physical examinations and pediatric care are provided, as are outpatient diagnostic services. The emphasis on preventive services, however, varies.
4. Plans have group centers where virtually all outpatient services are offered.
5. Physicians are in sole control of medical policy.

Kaiser Plans

In the Bay Area, there are Kaiser health plan facilities in all the counties but Sonoma. Affiliated with the plan are the Kaiser Foundation hospitals and medical care centers, and teams of doctors representing the major specialities of medicine. Nearly all the professional personnel practice within the program on a full-time basis. The physician groups work under a budget and are obligated to deliver all services on a contract basis. Thus, there are not only penalties for inefficiencies but a sharing of the saving from increased efficiency.*

At Kaiser Foundation medical facilities, all Kaiser plans provide a broad spectrum of services, from preventive through rehabilitative, by doctors associated with the plan. Provision is made for reimbursement up to a set amount for expenses incurred outside the service area in case of accident or emergency illness. Maintentenance of health as well as treatment of illness is stressed. Periodic health examinations are encouraged. Selection of a personal physician from among the medical staff is recommended.

---

*In California the contract also contains a feature, termed a "contingency contractual payment," that provides the medical groups with incentives to avoid lowering their costs by transferring expenses to Kaiser hospitals. The contract payment agreement of the health plan with the medical groups and the hospitals includes an added amount equal to 5 percent of total combined budgeted expenses. This amount is always divided equally between the two. The amount of the contingency payment is reduced to the extent that the hospitals run over their budgeted costs, and is increased to the extent that the hospital costs are under the budget. If medical group costs exceed the budgeted estimate, the difference is taken only from the physicians' share of the contingency payment, while the overall size of the payment remains the same. Thus, in order to insure the

SELF-INSURED PLANS

Some large employers assume full responsibility for administration and payment of claims under their employee health care plans. Alternatively, they may self-insure some of the coverages and partially insure others. Payment of all or the major portion of claims may be undertaken, with an insurance carrier underwriting the risk and/or being responsible for all other functions usually performed under a fully insured program.

The motivation for self-insurance usually arises from a belief that administration can be improved and that costs can be lowered through reduction or elimination of premiums, taxes, claim reserves, commission and various insurance carrier overhead charges.

SCOPE OF BENEFITS

The most comprehensive health care programs cover both inpatient and out-of-hospital services. Care in an extended care facility or convalescent home is one of the newer provisions in inpatient care. Among the

---

maintenance of physician income and the maximum incentive payment, the medical groups and the hospitals must cooperate in keeping costs low.

The medical group share of the incentive payment is divided equally among all partners of the group. Any overrun of the budget either by the medical group or the hospitals reduces the income of the partnership physicians. Conversely, the partners can increase their income by keeping expenses below budgeted costs--since with the exception of the contingency contractual payment, payments from the health plan to the medical group are fixed at the beginning of the year and are not changed if expenses fall below budgeted figures. (See U.S. National Advisory Commission on Health Manpower, *Health Care in America Report*, Vol. 11, Appendix IV, "The Kaiser Foundation Medical Care Program" (Washington, D.C.: 1967), pp. 197-228.

latest additions to out-of-hospital care is provision for home health services, such as part-time nursing care, home health aides and physical therapy. Such provisions are still infrequent.

Policies may or may not include care for dependents of the primary person insured. Inpatient benefits for dependents may be the same as for the primary person in some policies. Out-of-hospital benefits for dependents, however, may be less than for the primary person, or may not exist at all, except under major medical coverage. Dependents are usually defined as the spouse and dependent, unmarried children from the age of 14 days up to 18 years. Dependent children beyond age 18 who are physically or mentally handicapped may also be covered, as may dependent children to age 25 who are attending educational institutions.

Some policies specify that when an individual has more than one group health plan, combined payments from both plans will be provided up to but not to exceed 100 percent of charges for the actual services that are covered. Usually excluded from coverage are services provided through federal or state government, preexisting conditions, routine physical examinations, immunizations, and well-baby care, as well as such disabilities as venereal disease, self-inflicted injuries and illnesses, alcoholism and drug addiction. Coverage for treatment of mental illness is usually excluded from basic policies as is coverage for dental and vision care and prescription drugs.

Inpatient Benefits

Most hospitalization policies written today also include coverage for surgical expenses as well as other in-hospital services. Among them are:

Daily room and board charge. This covers accommodation in a semiprivate room (or three-bed ward) for a specified number of days, with payment in full or at a specified rate. Included are food service, routine nursing care and minor medical supplies.

Other charges. Covered separately are laboratory tests and x-rays provided in the hospital, anesthesia and its administration, drugs and medicines and use of the operating room. The limitation on this benefit may be expressed as the same number of days as for the daily room and board charge, or as a maximum dollar amount.

Registered physical therapist. Some basic policies include this service when rendered in the hospital up to the allowed number of hospital days.

X-ray therapy. X-ray, radium and radioactive isotope therapy may be provided at specified rates.

Maternity benefits. These are usually available in the form of a single lump-sum payment. They may be different for a primary insured and for a dependent. They may or may not include coverage for a normal delivery, but they usually provide for severe medical or surgical complications of pregnancy.

Surgery benefits. Services of a surgeon, assistant surgeon and anesthetist in indemnity insurance policies are usually compensated according to a fee schedule, frequently based in California on the California Medical Association's relative value scale expressed as a dollar value per unit.

Ambulance. Most policies provide coverage to and from the hospital in nonmaternity cases.

Convalescent care facility. Care in a skilled nursing home is beginning to be covered in basic policies. Each day of care counts for one-half day of hospital care.

Out-of-Hospital Benefits

Regular medical expense benefits ordinarily cover physician visits in the hospital but may also cover office and home visits.

Diagnostic outpatient x-ray and laboratory examinations are beginning to be covered in basic plans.

Payments for physician's care in indemnity plans are based on specified amounts per visit (usually one visit per day), or, as in newer policies, on the "usual, customary and reasonable" charge for similar physician services in the area. A maximum is usually set on the amount payable per year or per disability.

Other benefits. Major medical policies may partially reimburse the holder for special duty nursing in the hospital or at home, for outpatient prescription drugs and medicines, for blood transfusions, artificial limbs and rental of mechanical equipment, home care service and limited outpatient psychiatric care. This is in addition to picking up 75 or 80 percent (after deductible) of expenses in excess of those covered under the basic policy.

Comprehensive Health Plan Benefits

Hospitalization and out-of-hospital benefits are provided in a single program under comprehensive plans. In the Bay Area, the Kaiser Foundation Health Plan offers hospitalization varying from 60 to 150 days a year (depending upon group contract) and a wide range of outpatient services. All plans provide doctors' office and home visits, laboratory tests, x-ray therapy, casts and dressings, physical therapy, drugs, medicines, immunizations, injections, allergy tests, surgery, maternity care, vision care (except eyeglasses) and ambulance within the service area.

Neuromuscular rehabilitation services are provided at "health plan rates," said to be half prevailing rates. Charges for outpatient drug prescriptions filled at Kaiser facilities are either at "reasonable rates" or partially prepaid. No limit is placed on number of office or home visits. A charge is made for the first two home visits at $3.50 from 9 a.m. to 5 p.m. and $5 from 5 p.m. to 9 a.m.

Prepaid benefits specifically exclude from coverage mental illness or disorders,* tuberculosis, poliomyelitis, custodial or convalescent care, cosmetic surgery, dental care, podiatry, alcoholism, and drug addiction, corrective appliances and artificial aids.

Although all Kaiser contracts reflect the above provisions, they vary in detail. For example, there are nine different drug codes, nine maternity codes and 13 dependent codes. Contracts also differ in length of hospital benefit and in charges made for office visits. Under each type of coverage, there are also differences in charges for outpatient drugs, in out-of-area benefits and in possible psychiatric benefits.

Group programs may combine one type of plan for the primary insured with a different type for the dependent, or may select the same type of plan for both primary insured and dependents.

THE NEWER INSURANCE COVERAGES

One reason that people covered by health insurance have substantial out-of-pocket costs--apart from ceilings on reimbursement, deductibles and copayment--is that so many facets of medical care have been considered uninsurable. Most basic health care programs--including both indemnity and service plans--still explicitly exclude from coverage dental work (except as necessary in case of an accident), eye refractions and the cost of glasses,

---

*Some Kaiser contracts do provide limited psychiatric benefits. See, for example, section on collectively bargained health care plans, pp. 49-66.

hearing aids and the fitting thereof, treatment of mental disorders, corrective appliances and artificial aids, prescription drugs outside the hospital, treatment of alcoholism or drug addiction, as well as treatment of pulmonary tuberculosis.

Consumer demand for coverage of dental care and prescription drugs has been growing in recent years, as has the demand for some protection against the costs of psychiatric treatment. Insurance companies and special professional groups have been slowly responding to this demand, as described below.

Dental Care

Pilot programs operated by dental service corporations in the last decade have proved that dental insurance is workable on a group basis. The number of group dental care plans being adopted is growing rapidly, and indications are that this trend will continue. Nationwide, about 5 million persons are covered for such care, about one-fourth of them in California.

The typical insured plan provides a fairly broad schedule of benefits including periodic oral examinations, x-rays, cleaning, extractions, inlays, bridgework, dentures, oral surgery, anesthesia, treatment of gum diseases and root canal therapy. Orthodontia is usually excluded but may be included under a supplemental premium. Benefits cover 70 to 75 percent of cost, according to a fixed schedule of maximum allowances. Most plans set a ceiling on the total amount reimbursable for a year. The cost of preexisting conditions is usually covered.

Union labor plans. The component of dental care in group health plans owes its momentum to collective bargaining agreements. The first major dental care plan negotiated in California was the program for children established under an agreement between the International Longshoremen's and Warehousemen's Union and the

Pacific Maritime Association in 1954. Every child up to age 15 who is dependent for support on a man eligible for ILWU-PMA welfare fund benefits is entitled to dental benefits. All dental services are covered except orthodontia.

By mid-1968 the Teamsters Union had negotiated dental care plans for more California workers than any other union. Seven unions accounted for 85 percent of workers with dental coverage: Teamsters, Retail Clerks, Hotel and Restaurant Employees and Bartenders, Carpenters, Butchers, Plumbers, Longshoremen and Warehousemen. Industries covered include unionized employers in construction, retail food and liquor stores, eating and drinking places, hotel and other lodging places, food and kindred products manufacturing, motor freight transportation and warehousing, canning and preserving fruits, vegetables and seafoods, retail trade (except automobile), wholesale trade, water transportation and miscellaneous industries.[10] Automobile and aerospace industry workers' agreements negotiated in 1967 include dental care in health programs for 1969 and 1970.

Plan underwriters. Dental care programs are underwritten by commercial insurance companies, by Blue Shield as a rider to basic group policies and by professional groups. Included in addition to the insurance carriers in the Bay Area are the California Dental Service, sponsored by the California Dental Association, and the Naismith Dental Group, a closed panel plan.

The California Dental Service (a Delta Dental Plan) provides for the free choice of any licensed dentist. It offers an incentive to dental health by raising the proportion of reimbursable charges from 70 to 80 percent in the second year for individuals and families who visit the dentist at least once during the first year of coverage and undergo all prescribed treatment. For such subscribers the Dental Service assumes 90 percent of the allowed charges during the third year and 100 percent during all subsequent years. If during any

12-month period of eligibility a person fails to visit a dentist and have all prescribed care, the portion that the Dental Service will pay for him reverts to 70 percent. Reimbursement for prosthetics (including such items as dentures and bridges) is 50 percent and does not change from year to year.

The Naismith group provides prepaid dental care only at its own facilities. Membership is available both to individuals and to groups. Group coverage varies, depending on the contract. For example, Naismith in 1969 contracted with a collectively bargained health and welfare fund to provide $300 worth of dental care per family per contract year without charge to the member; 70 percent of charges in excess of $300 up to $700 per family per year; 20 percent of charges over $700 per family per year.

Prescription Drugs

The cost of drugs is one of the major items in illness, sometimes equaling the cost of physician's services. Inclusion of this benefit in a health care plan has therefore been growing. The Health Insurance Institute estimates that about 70 million Americans under age 65 have some form of insurance or prepayment against the cost of prescribed drugs. These include 60 million with commercial major medical policies and about 9.6 million with Blue Shield-Blue Cross extended benefit certificates.[11] The Health Insurance Institute does not mention pharmacist-sponsored organizations specializing in providing drug benefits, such as California Paid Prescriptions, an affiliate of California Pharmaceutical Service.

Plans in effect normally cover only prescription drugs, with the subscriber paying a small charge for each prescription and the plan paying the balance up to a maximum amount such as the "going" price in the area. Most plans exclude coverage of contraceptives, vitamins and dietary supplements, injectable drugs, blood and blood plasma.

Negotiated health plans pioneered in the area of insurance for prescription drugs. Some health and welfare trust funds are self-insured for prescription drugs; that is, they pay the pharmacist's claim directly or reimburse the member. The California Department of Industrial Relations estimates that in mid-1968 about 325,000 California workers had outpatient prescription drug coverage provided through collective bargaining agreements. Six unions accounted for 94 percent of the workers in the state with this coverage. They were Retail Clerks, Teamsters, Hotel and Restaurant Employees and Bartenders, Carpenters, Laborers, and Butchers. Negotiated coverage for automobile workers and garment workers became effective in 1969, adding about 30,000 workers.[12]

Under one collectively bargained welfare fund in the Bay Area, an eligible member is reimbursed 75 to 85 percent of cost after a $10 deductible, applied every six months. Under another contract, eligible members pay $1.25 for each prescription, and the remaining cost is covered by insurance. Still another health and welfare trust fund reimburses eligible members 90 percent of the usual and customary prices of Bay Area drugstores.

Vision Care

Vision care, except for necessary surgery, is another service ordinarily omitted from health care plans. At present this benefit is largely limited to employees represented by unions, and the total number covered is relatively small. Commercial carriers insure vision care under major medical contracts. In the Bay Area, services are also written by California Vision Services, sponsored by the California Optometric Association. Benefits include screening, vision analysis and refractions. Some plans also provide for filling lens prescriptions and for frames.

An example of 1970 coverage is the Sheet Metal Workers Trust Fund which provides $10 for screening, $20 for refractions and not more than an additional $15 for lenses and $15 for frames, with a maximum of $50 every two years. This benefit applies to employees only and not to dependents. Also, the Northern California Teamsters' local unions provide for both eligible members and dependents a vision care plan that includes vision analysis and lenses every 12 months and frames every two years, on a reimbursable basis according to a schedule of allowances. Reimbursement for frames is limited to $8.

Psychiatric Coverage

For psychiatric care, insurance coverage is still relatively low. It is far less extensive than for other illnesses in general hospitals, and less extensive in public than in private mental hospitals. Coverage is often limited to a given number of days, and sometimes it covers only a few days in the lifetime of the subscriber.

A highly relevant factor in this inadequate coverage has been the limited public demand for its provision. All past broadening of health insurance has been in response to demand, but a substantial demand for psychiatric coverage and a willingness to pay for it have not yet been felt. As one expert in the field says, "People never expect to become mentally ill." On the other hand, the use of new drugs and a growing emphasis on the value of early treatment have spurred the trend toward community care and have been potent in stimulating interest. Coverage for psychiatric conditions is growing and will increase as demand rises.

Federal Employees and Mental Health Benefits

This is the largest single employer-sponsored health insurance plan in the world. From its beginning in 1960, it has included some psychiatric coverage, and renegotiation of the program each year has brought additional prepayment plans into some psychiatric coverage and led others into improving this benefit.

The Blue Cross-Blue Shield Service Benefit Plan, the largest of the government-wide plans, the Aetna Indemnity Benefit Plan and Kaiser Foundation Health Plan in California all now provide both in-hospital and out-of-hospital coverage for mental illness.

Unions and Psychiatric Coverage

Union labor is also becoming somewhat more interested in psychiatric coverage. Until recently most union negotiators for health plans were not convinced of the importance of including psychiatric services, chiefly, perhaps, because they were giving priority to securing other health benefits, such as dental care and reduced cost of drugs. Also, many unionists feared that disclosure of treatment for a psychiatric condition would prejudice employers.

Many unions, however, have begun to press for mental health benefits. The Retail Clerks Local 770 in Los Angeles won provision for psychiatric treatment in its 1959 contract. Contracts negotiated by the International Union of Automobile Workers in 1964 won psychiatric insurance for its members, with employers paying the full premiums as part of overall health insurance coverage. The benefit program, designed with the assistance of the American Psychiatric Association and the National Institute of Mental Health, was negotiated with 16 major corporations in the automobile and agricultural implement industries, and began operation in the fall of 1966. It was the first nationally negotiated basic coverage psychiatric insurance.

Essentially similar coverage has been negotiated by unions with employers in the aerospace industry and in the steel, aluminum and can industries. Most employers in these industries have extended the coverage to their nonbargaining unit employees.

Psychiatric Care Study: 1967

The American Psychiatric Association and the National Association for Mental Health, in a 1967 study, found that 61 percent of the patients in reporting hospitals had insurance policies that paid some part of their bills. The average proportion of the bill paid in voluntary general hospitals was 71 percent, and in private psychiatric hospitals 58 percent. The number of patients with Blue Cross coverage was about equal to the number with commercial insurance.[13]

Of patients treated outside the hospital, a much smaller proportion was covered by insurance--only 26 percent nationwide. For California the estimate was 22 percent.[14] The study pointed out that

> Insurers and employers purchasing group insurance increasingly seem to recognize that short term intensive psychiatric treatment is a necessary and sound service for employees. Insurers and the public both need to be made more aware that early diagnosis and out of hospital treatment, combined as necessary with partial hospitalization or brief stays in a general hospital, can be demonstrated to ward off prolonged, expensive stays in psychiatric hospitals.[15]

Health plans that cover psychiatric care ordinarily exclude treatment of alcoholism. However, the Health Insurance Institute believes that this exclusion is now being reappraised by both management and union officials. The Institute states, "Industry sources have claimed that the alcoholic worker, denied recourse to treatment under his employer group health insurance, is prone to abuse the company's sick leave or sick pay plan, with a consequent estimated workday loss of 22 days per year for the problem drinker and his company." The Institute further points out that one force leading to reappraisal is psychiatric diagnosis of alcoholism as symptomatic of mental illness.[16]

TERMINATION OF BENEFITS

At this point it is pertinent to stress that for all the many advantages inherent in group insurance plans, the member is covered only so long as he remains a member of the group. When his employment ceases, his group insurance also ceases, although he often has the privilege of converting to an individual policy without medical certification.

Benefits under individual policies, however, are usually lower and premiums higher than under the group plan. The jobless person, moreover, is apt to want to economize on his expenditures, particularly in periods of high unemployment, and thus often does not convert to the individual policy.

Most group insurance policies stipulate that sickness and accident insurance terminate at the end of the month last worked or 31 days after the month last worked. Some health and welfare funds carry members with some seniority a little longer, and some provide that under certain circumstances members may themselves pay into the welfare fund for designated periods. Examples of various provisions follow:

International Brotherhood of Teamsters/California Packing House Employees and Warehousemen's Unions Health and Welfare Plan.

> The insurance of the individual shall automatically terminate on... the date of expiration of the period for which the last premium

> payment is made on account of the individual's insurance....
>
> If the individual fails to work the required number of hours because of... layoff...he may continue his insurance in force for successive one-month periods up to a maximum of six months commencing with the date on which his insurance would otherwise terminate provided...he pays the required premium contribution one month in advance during the first five days of each month during which the insurance is so continued....
>
> An employee whose insurance terminates for any reason may have issued to him without medical examination an individual policy of insurance, provided application is made and premium paid...thirty-one days after the termination of insurance.

Similar provisions are made under many other contracts for participants in the Teamsters Security Fund.

San Francisco Lithographers Welfare Fund. Coverage ends one month after termination of employment cr after the month for which a contribution has been paid, whichever is later. For unemployed members who have participated in the welfare fund for 36 or more calendar months coverage continues for a maximum of three months; for those who have participated for 60 or more months, coverage continues for a maximum of six months. In order to qualify for continuation of coverage, members must show that they are actively seeking and available for work in the industry.

Railway Labor Organizations National Group Insurance Plan. Health insurance benefits of qualifying employees on furlough (layoff) end the fourth month following the month in which compensated service was rendered, or the employee received vacation pay. Where the employment relationship is actually terminated, benefits end on termination date.

California Metal Trades Association/International Association of Machinists Joint Health and Welfare Trust. The insurance of an employee terminates on the last day of the month in which his employment terminates.

> However, if termination of employment is due to cessation of an employer's business operations, leave of absence or temporary layoff, the insurance may be continued for a period not exceeding twelve (12) months if the employee pays the full premium monthly on or before the first day of each month to his employer.

Automotive Industries Welfare Fund. Eligible employees who are temporarily laid off may self-pay full premiums for up to three months. Some agreements cover the employee for 31 days after he becomes ineligible. Others terminate him at the end of the month in which he leaves employment.

Northern California Retail Clerks/Employers Welfare Trust Fund. Maintenance of eligibility for benefits requires 65 hours of employment in each calendar month. Eligibility ends on the last day of the second month after the last month with the required number of hours worked. If the standard is not met because of unemployment, coverage may be maintained by self-payments into the fund for as long as six months, provided the member is unemployed and available for work in the industry.

Other funds. Provision for self-payment into the welfare fund for specified periods is also made by, among others, the Oakland Restaurant and Tavern Welfare Fund, San Francisco Culinary, Bartenders and Service Employees Welfare Fund, Carpenters Health and Welfare Trust Fund and Sheet Metal Workers Welfare Plan.

CHAPTER *II*

Health Care Plans in Bay Area Industry

Protection against the costs of medical care is provided for various groups in the Bay Area as in other urban areas of the state and the nation. A substantial proportion of employees in private industry, especially those working for larger employers, are covered by group health care programs attained through collective bargaining or administrative decision. Replies to a questionnaire on company health care programs revealed some coverage by every type of plan described in the preceding chapter.

More than 90 (91.2) percent of the 488 industry respondents reported their employees were covered by a company-sponsored health care plan. The others were chiefly small firms: 7 out of 8 with fewer than 25 employees.

Almost 3 out of 10 plans analyzed (29 percent) pertained to salaried workers alone, either because there were no wage workers in the Bay Area location of the respondent or because he had no information on the composition of the health care plan covering unionized wage workers. A negotiated health plan covered almost all unionized workers in firms of 100 or more in the San Francisco Bay Area.[1] Here it is relevant to note that although labor unions set the pace both for initiating and broadening health and welfare benefits, favorable tax provisions have spread these benefits to salaried and nonunion workers. Asked whether their health care programs had originated in a collective bargaining agreement, over half the respondents (56 percent) indicated that they had, in whole or in part.

WHO HAS WHAT?

Studies by the U.S. Bureau of Labor Statistics indicate that in 1969 similar percentages of plant and office workers were in Bay Area establishments that had formal health care plans covering hospital and surgical benefits, but that a somewhat higher proportion of salaried workers had medical expense benefits and major medical insurance.[2]

Many industrial respondents to the questionnaire had multiple union contracts. Fifteen percent of them declared that they had no information about plans covering their hourly workers. Typical responses on this subject were:

> Under the terms of our union contract we make payments to the Health Trust who administer the plan. Payments are based on the number of hours each employee works during the preceding month. We have no control and very little information on the benefits involved. We do know that the union members have their choice of coverage under either the CPS [California Physicians Service] or Kaiser Foundation Health Plan, but we do not know who or how many are covered. The hourly contribution we make is the same regardless of whether the employee is single or married with any number of dependents.
>
> . . . . .
>
> Answers to questions cover salaried personnel only. Hourly coverage is reflected under various building trade unions which have separately administered benefit payments.

One large industrial firm reported 24 health plans in effect, 22 of them with indemnity insurance companies and 2 with the Blues. Another firm had eight plans covering 600 employees, and one large food products firm was gracious enough to send copies of six plans, each covering different occupational groups. One respondent with only 12 workers paid into two different union health funds at two different rates per man-hour.

Newspaper publishers were among those with multiple union agreements who did not know the details of employee health plans. Only one of the 13 from whom information was requested filled out the questionnaire, and the reply dealt only with "nonbargaining" employees. Said this respondent, "We contribute to 18 trust accounts for bargaining employees, and we do not have information on their plans." Similar responses came from two others, while a third said:

> This company provides medical and hospital insurance, including major medical, for employees represented in collective bargaining by a number of unions. Specifically we have ten agreements, all of which simply provide for our payment of specified sums of money into welfare funds administered by representatives of the various unions and the San Francisco newspapers. We do not even have copies of the medical and hospital plans in many cases.

A number of respondents who indicated that their firm had a health care plan for employees were reluctant to communicate the details because they deemed the questions an invasion of their privacy, a thought that had not occurred to the researcher. One respondent returned the schedule with a note: "The best health insurance you can get is to do some *work*. Please try it and stop spending my hard earned money on these good for nothing programs," and signed it "Fed-up."

UNDERWRITERS

Commercial indemnity insurance companies were principal underwriters of the 445 health care plans described by respondents. The majority of the employees in 71 percent of the responding firms were covered by commercial insurance.* This figure may be understated since so many respondents did not report the plans of their unionized employees, and many of the large health and welfare trust funds are underwritten by commercial carriers.

Blue Cross and Blue Shield underwrote 18 percent of the plans reported, and one percent were self-insured. Five percent of the respondents indicated that most employees were covered by a union-management health and welfare trust fund.

Five percent of the respondents indicated that most of their employees were covered by a comprehensive prepayment plan such as Kaiser's. However, an additional 13 percent indicated that a portion of their employees were covered by the Kaiser plan.**

EMPLOYER CONTRIBUTION

Employers paid the entire health insurance premium for both salaried and hourly workers in 4 out of 5 reported plans. In about half the plans, insurance premiums for employee and dependents were fully paid by the employer. Hourly workers were somewhat better off

---

*Respondents were asked to describe the plan that covered the majority of their employees.

**The California Department of Industrial Relations found in 1965 that 10 percent of negotiated plans in California firms were covered by Kaiser. See California Department of Industrial Relations, Division of Labor Statistics and Research, *California Industrial Relations Reports*, No. 29 (1967), Table 4, p. 25.

than salaried employees in that the total premium, including coverage for the family, was employer paid in 56 percent of the plans, compared with 45 percent for salaried employees.

No employer contribution to the health plan costs for either salaried or hourly workers was made in 2 percent of the reported plans. No part of the premium cost for dependents was employer paid in a quarter of the reported plans. The following table brings out some of the differences in the employer contribution for salaried and hourly workers in plans for which this information was given.

Percent of Health Plan Premium Paid by Employer

Health plans	Salaried employees Employee	Salaried employees Dependent	Hourly employees Employee	Hourly employees Dependent
Number	417	417	354	354
Percent	100.0	100.0	100.0	100.0
Percent paid				
100	80.0	44.8	87.1	56.0
50 - 90	16.6	22.1	9.8	14.6
Under 50	1.5	4.1	1.4	2.0
None	1.9	29.0	1.7	27.4

Almost 3 out of every 4 plans provided similar benefits for employee and dependents. Lesser benefits for dependents usually omitted outpatient care. Children were covered to age 19 in most plans, although many included them to age 23 if they were still at school and dependent.

HEALTH PLAN BENEFITS

Besides the basic health care plan, 17 out of every 25 respondents stated that their programs automatically included a major medical policy that paid 70 to 80 percent of specified medical costs after a deductible amount. Benefits either not covered by the basic plan or expenditures in excess of collectable amounts under the basic plan were thus reimbursed. Major medical was not offered to employees in 4 out of 25 plans.

One out of every 25 firms offered major medical as an option--usually entirely at the employee's expense. Major medical alone served as the basic plan in 3 out of 25 plans. The health care programs that offered major medical in lieu of a basic plan and those that consisted only of a basic plan without major medical were both found chiefly in firms employing fewer than 25 employees.

Hospitalization

All 415 basic plans covered hospital daily service charges and other hospital charges. Almost 70 percent provided a specific number of days in a three-bed ward or semiprivate room, either paid in full or at a fixed sum per day.* In the 283 plans based on this method, 62 percent paid full cost for 20 to 365 days, the most frequent periods being 70 to 100 days.

A limitation both on reimbursable charges and on the number of hospital days was found in 38 percent of the plans reported. The maximum on charges ranged from lows of $10, $12, and $14 a day (for 90, 70 and 30 days respectively) to a high of $60 (for 70 days). Virtually every figure between these two extremes was mentioned in some plan as a ceiling on reimbursement for hospital daily charges. The levels most often mentioned were $30 to $39 in 7 out of 20 plans, and $40 to $49 in 5 out of 20. The maximum in 2 out of 20 plans was $50, with

---

*In some plans, usually for persons below a certain income level and usually under Blue Cross, the hospital is paid directly by the insurer.

a higher ceiling in one out of 20. Five out of 20 plans paid under $30 a day; 2 of these paid $20 or less.

None of the plans reported covered hospital care for fewer than 20 days. Two percent covered for 20 or 21 days and 8 percent for 365. The number of days' hospital coverage provided by these 283 plans was as follows:

Days of coverage	Percent of plans	
20 - 21	2	
30 - 31	14	
35 - 60	4	
70	24	
90	2	
100	25	
111	6	
120	11	
150 - 240	4	
365	8	
	100	Total

On the other hand, about 30 percent of the basic plans avoided the device of limiting the number of days, or the daily cost for which reimbursement is available for hospital daily charges. Instead, they incorporated a dollar or percentage ceiling on total daily hospital service charges, or on total reimbursable costs per single episode of illness, or on all sums collectable under the policy maximum. In addition to daily room and board charges, hospitals bill for use of operating

---

*Since the 1969 average hospital daily charge in the Bay Area was around $80 for a semiprivate room, it is clear that individuals who are not members of basic plans providing service benefits could be faced with sizable out-of-pocket expenditures in case of serious illness, even if they are also covered by a major medical policy.

rooms, laboratory and x-ray tests and therapy, anesthesia, medication, dressings, blood, oxygen, and so on, all subsumed under "other charges." The reported limitations on other charges differed so widely that no attempt was made to summarize them. Suffice it to say that few plans covered them in full; some paid a few hundred dollars and some a few thousand, or a percentage of costs after a specified sum.

Surgical Benefits

Not all *basic plans* covered surgical bills, but cost of surgery was reimbursed in these plans under a supplemental *major medical policy*. Except where benefits were on a service basis, as in some Blues contracts and the Kaiser system, reimbursement for surgical benefits varied according to a fixed schedule for different procedures. For a few plans, particularly in the major medical portion, reimbursement for surgical costs was reported on the basis of "reasonable and customary charges."

Physician Visits

Coverage of physician visits, known as medical expense insurance, has been the last of the types of insurance to be included in basic health care plans. Physician hospital visits are more commonly provided than are office calls or home visits. The 405 basic plans for which information was given on this item furnished hospital visits almost twice as often as office calls. Major medical policies, however, covered both in-hospital and out-of-hospital physician services in most plans. Only 5 percent of the health care plans reported made no provision for physician services. The following table shows the availability of such services in the reported plans.

Type Plan	Hospital		Office		Home	
	No.	%	No.	%	No.	%
All plans	405	100	405	100	405	100
Basic	248	61	130	32	120	30
Major medical	142	35	250	62	250	62
No provision	15	4	25	6	35	8

Coverage under major medical involves payment by the plan member of a fixed deductible per year plus 20 to 30 percent of the physician's charge.

Hospital Visits

Provision for physician visits in the hospital was made by 61 percent of the basic plans reviewed. In three-fifths of these plans a dollar ceiling was placed on the reimbursable portions of the physician's fee. This ran from $3 a visit in 13 percent of the plans to $12 and $15 in 7 percent. In 73 percent, the top reimbursement for a physician's hospital visit was $4, $5 and $6, with the largest concentration at $5. Physician hospital fees in the other 7 percent of the plans ranged from $7 to $10 a visit with no concentration at any one point. Virtually all plans paid for a specified number of visits, usually the same as the reimbursable number of hospital days.

Physician visits in the hospital were provided under major medical in an additional 35 percent of the plans reviewed. Four of the plans reported, however, made no provision at all for this service.

Office Visits

Provision for physician office visits was made in only 32 percent of the basic plans. Major medical policies, however, covered out-of-hospital physician services in an additional 62 percent of the plans.

Where cost of physician office visits was included in the basic plan, top reimbursement ranged from $3 to $6 a visit. Nine out of 10 plans incorporated this ceiling, with 6 out of 10 setting the limit at $4 and $5. From $7 to $10 per visit was paid by 1 plan in 10. Although some plans limited the number of office visits that could be reimbursed under the policy, most stipulated the total amount that would be paid for a single disability or calendar year.

Most basic plans specified that charges for office calls would not be reimbursed for the first two visits in case of illness, although reimbursement from the first visit would be paid for accidental injuries. Some plans included office visits for the employee but not for his dependents. Higher reimbursement was not provided for office visits encompassing complete diagnostic examinations.

Home Visits

In 8 percent of the health care plans reviewed, no provision was made for physician visits in the home. Less than a third provided for such visits in the basic plan, and under most plans, where the benefit was provided, the cost of the first two visits for illness was not reimbursed. Some plans excluded dependents from this benefit.

Reimbursement for house calls was usually somewhat higher than for office calls, with almost 60 percent paying $5 and $6 per visit, and 25 percent paying $10 or more. Here, too, a ceiling was set on the total amount that could be reimbursed for a single illness or a calendar year.

NEWER BENEFITS IN INDUSTRY PLANS

Many of the newer benefits in health care programs, discussed in the preceding chapter, were found in Bay Area plans, according to information made available by 408 respondents. A benefit covering some psychiatric care was reported by 66 percent, prescription drugs by more than half, and dental care by 25 percent. Vision care coverage was reported by almost 10 percent.

Psychiatric Care

Nine in every 25 plans specifically excluded psychiatric care; 11 provided care both in the hospital and out of the hospital; and 5 covered only hospitalization. Lack of coverage occurred principally in firms with fewer than 50 employees.

One in 25 firms that reported full coverage stated that benefits for mental illness were the same as for physical illness. Of the health care plans that included only hospitalization for mental illness, 10 out of 25 reported that benefits equalled those for physical illness.

Where out-of-hospital psychiatric care was covered, it was usually provided under a major medical plan. Maximum reimbursement for the calendar year was generally set at $500, with a lifetime maximum established at $1000. Reimbursement for physician's office visits was limited to 50 a year with 50 percent coinsurance to a top of $10 a visit, with the usual deductible.

Some basic plans that did not specifically exclude psychiatric care did indeed provide the same benefits as for other medical care, but the top reimbursement for a physician's office visit was $3 to $5.

Prescription Drugs

An out-of-hospital prescription drug benefit was provided in 65 percent of the health care plans for which this information was reported. In 4 out of 5 cases it was a component of a major medical policy, with cost reimbursable at 70 to 80 percent after the stipulated deductible. Reported plans that included partially paid prescription drugs as a benefit under a basic health care program were underwritten chiefly by the Kaiser Foundation Health Plan.

Some employees in respondent firms were covered for prescription drugs under union-management health and welfare trust funds that contracted separate policies, frequently written by Paid Prescriptions, an affiliate of California Pharmaceutical Service.

Dental Care

One out of 4 respondents indicated a dental benefit as a component of the firm's health care program, usually under a separate contract.* In 15 percent of these plans, the benefit was available only to employees covered by a collective bargaining agreement.

Vision Care

Only 2 out of 25 respondents reported a vision care benefit that covered screening, vision analysis and refractions. A ceiling was placed on each procedure and on the maximum payable within a specified period. Almost 15 percent of the plans were available only under union-management negotiated plans, which usually include eyeglasses when necessary.

---

*One respondent indicated that his company paid 65 percent of the premium for its health care plan, but 100 percent of the premium for dental care.

Half the vision care provisions reported were a component of the Kaiser Foundation plan. This program excludes provision of eyeglasses. The remaining vision care benefits were provided either through major medical contracts or California Vision Services.

COLLECTIVELY BARGAINED HEALTH CARE PLANS

Collectively bargained health care plans cover half the persons in private industry programs. Health and welfare trust funds, set up jointly by employers and unions, administer various health insurance plans not only for active employees and their dependents but also for retired employees and dependents. Benefits for retired members age 65 and over usually supplement federal Medicare. In addition, the trust funds have responsibility for other group insurance plans: life, accidental death and dismemberment, retirement, sick leave, vacations and sometimes a "sabbatical leave" benefit.* Benefits may be financed solely by employers who contribute an agreed upon amount per employee per hour worked or on a contributory basis with employees sharing the cost.

The trust funds may contract with more than one type of underwriter--a commercial insurance company, the Blues or a group-practice plan--in order to afford members dual or multiple choice of coverage. They may also contract separately for dental or vision services for their members, or for payment of out-of-hospital prescription drugs.

---

*The California cannery industry and the California State Council of Cannery and Food Processing Unions, International Brotherhood of Teamsters, for example, have set up a sabbatical leave trust under which an employee with 15 years regular seniority is entitled to nine consecutive weeks of time off once each five years, with leave payment equal to 360 hours' pay. This is in addition to regular vacation pay.

Unions that have agreements with different industries may set up joint trust funds with employers in each of those industries. The San Francisco Joint Board of Culinary Workers, Bartenders, and Hotel and Restaurant Employees International Union, for example, negotiates with four employer associations each of which has its own health and welfare trust fund. The International Longshoremen's and Warehousemen's Union participates in a trust fund for longshoremen with the Pacific Maritime Association, and in one for warehousemen in the Distributors Association Hospital and Medical Trust. On the other hand, the International Brotherhood of Teamsters, Chauffeurs, Warehousemen and Helpers participates in the Teamsters Security Fund, which administers health care programs for a number of different industrial groups.

Principal joint trust funds in the Bay Area whose medical care plans were examined for this study were the Automotive Industries Welfare Fund; Carpenters Health and Welfare Trust Fund; California Metal Trades Association/International Association of Machinists Joint Health and Welfare Trust; International Longshoremen's and Warehousemen's Union/Pacific Maritime Association Welfare Fund; ILWU/Warehousemen and Distributors Association Hospital and Medical Trust; Northern California Retail Clerks/Employers Welfare Trust Fund; Northern California Teamsters Security Fund; Oakland Restaurant and Tavern Welfare Fund; San Francisco Culinary, Bartenders and Service Employees Welfare Fund; San Francisco Lithographers Welfare Fund; Sheet Metal Workers Welfare Plan of Northern California; United Steel Workers of America.

Automotive Industries Welfare Fund

Trustees of this joint welfare fund represent the following employers and unions: Automotive Industries, Inc.; East Bay Automotive Jobbers Association, Inc.; Richmond Motor Car Dealers Association; Southern Alameda County Motor Car Dealers Association; California Trucking Association, Inc.; and other participating employers who are parties to this fund by agreement with: Automotive Machinists Lodge 1546; Automotive Teamsters Local 78; Automotive Painters Local 1176; East Bay Automotive Council on behalf of its affiliates; and Northern California Automotive Machinists Council, on behalf of its affiliates and other participating unions.

Eligible employees may choose an indemnity plan with free choice of hospital and physician, underwritten by Occidental Life Insurance Company or the Kaiser Foundation service plan.

Principal Occidental benefits. The indemnity plan covers identical in-hospital and diagnostic laboratory and x-ray benefits for employees and dependents and home and office physician visits for the employee only. Reimbursement for hospitalization is $27 per day for room and board charges up to 70 days and 100 percent up to $300 of other charges plus 75 percent of additional expense incurred.

Surgery is covered in accord with the CMA relative value study with no dollar maximum per disability. Physician's home and office visits for the employee are reimbursed at $7.50 and $5 per day up to $375 during any six consecutive months.

Psychiatric conditions are treated in the same way as any other condition requiring medical attention.

Principal Kaiser benefits. The Kaiser plan provides the same benefits for employees and dependents: 111 days' hospitalization, surgery, unlimited doctor's office and hospital visits and diagnostic procedures, all at no charge. Doctor's home visits carry a charge of $3.50 (or $5 after 5 p.m.) for the first two calls and no charge thereafter. Doctor's care includes eye examinations and refractions, as well as other diagnosis and treatment, and routine physical checkups. Psychiatric conditions are not covered.

Carpenters Health and Welfare Trust Fund

Eligible carpenters may choose coverage under Blue Cross or the Kaiser Foundation. In addition to hospital, surgical and medical expense benefits, carpenters are covered for dental care and outpatient prescription drugs. Inpatient and outpatient psychiatric care are excluded from both Blue Cross and Kaiser plans.

Blue Cross pays the hospital directly for care in a room of three or more beds at the full rate for all services. Surgical and medical bills and those for diagnostic laboratory and x-ray and radium therapy benefits are sent to Blue Cross which then mails to the subscriber (eligible employee) a check made payable both to subscriber and physician.

All benefits except physician's office and home visits cover the employee and eligible dependents. Out-of-hospital physician services cover employees only. Maximum payable physician fee is $4 for office visits and $5 for home calls. Benefits begin with first visit as a result of an accident and third as a result of illness, up to $300 in a calendar year. Chiropractic is covered at $4 per visit up to 12 visits each calendar year.

Kaiser Foundation Health Plan provides equal benefits for employee and dependents. Benefits cover 111 days' hospitalization, laboratory tests, x-ray tests and therapy, and surgery all at no charge. Physician office visits cost $1 per visit and home calls $3.50 (or $5 evening) for the first two visits, with no charge thereafter. Medical care includes periodic checkups and eye examinations.

Drug benefits. Carpenters subscribing to the Kaiser plan pay reduced rates for all outpatient prescription drugs purchased at a Kaiser facility.

Subscribers to Blue Cross are covered for outpatient prescription drugs under a trust fund plan that is self-insured. Only the primary insured and not the dependent is entitled to this benefit. Eligible employees pay $1.50 for each prescription or refill, and the fund pays any excess of that amount. Prescriptions must be filled through a participating pharmacy.

CMTA/IAM Joint Health and Welfare Trust

California Metal Trades Association/International Association of Machinists group insurance, underwritten by the Union Labor Life Insurance Company, provides reimbursement for in-hospital services, surgery and doctor's calls, as well as nonhospital laboratory tests and x-ray and treatment for eligible employees and their dependents. Doctors' home and office calls are reimbursed for employees only. Dependents include children between the ages of 19 and 23 who rely entirely upon the employee for support, and older children who are dependent because of mental or physical handicap.

Reimbursements include hospital room and board and other services at full cost in a three-bed ward for 100 days; cost of surgery in line with a fee schedule to a maximum of $1200 for one disability; and physician hospital visits at $6 per day. Maternity benefits are similar for employee and dependent. There is no maximum on laboratory and x-ray tests or treatment in case of accident, but there is a ceiling of $300 in any 12-month period in case of illness. Reimbursement for home or office medical treatment, for the employee only, is set at $6 for office visits and $12 per home call ($18 after 8 p.m.), up to 100 visits in a calendar year. Benefits begin with first visit in case of accident and third visit in case of illness. Treatment for mental illness is not specifically excluded from coverage.

ILWU/PMA Welfare Fund

The International Longshoremen's and Warehousemen's Union/Pacific Maritime Association Fund provides hospital-medical-surgical benefits and children's dental services* for eligible employees and their dependents. The choice offered is an indemnity plan underwritten by Pacific National Life Assurance Company or a service plan under Kaiser.

Although dependents are covered under both plans, maximum reimbursement for many services under the indemnity plan is less for dependents than for the employee. For example, only half the maximum for hospital room and board payable for the employee is available for a dependent. The maximum of $1925 for the employee and $962.50 for the dependent at $27.50 a day works out at 70 and 35 days reimbursable hospitalization. For other hospital charges the maximum reimbursable is $500 for employee and $350 for dependents. The difference between $27.50 and the actual charge per day is borne by the employee as in other insurance contracts. The maximum reimbursable for surgery is $600. Reimbursement is made according to a fee schedule based on the CMA relative value study.**

Physician's hospital visits are reimbursed at $5 per day both for the primary insured and the dependent; for office visits at $5 for the primary insured and $3 for the dependent; and house calls at $7.50 and $5 per visit. Reimbursement for out-of-hospital visits for dependents begins with the first visit for each injury and the second for each illness. Maximum reimbursement for maternity care is $125 for physician's fee and $125 for hospital for normal delivery; twice those amounts for Caesarean delivery; and half for an interrupted pregnancy.

The indemnity plan does not pay for routine physical checkups or for immunizations.

---

*See pp. 27-28 for description of this plan.

**Relative value study: Fees are based on units of service. The California Medical Association has selected a simple service as the basic unit and the relative value scale expresses more complex or lengthy services as multiples of that unit.

Principal benefits of the Kaiser Foundation plan for ILWU/PMA members serviced by Kaiser hospitals and health plan professional staff are 111 days' hospitalization and surgery and unlimited physician office visits at no charge, among other services. Physician's home visits are charged at $2 for the first visit. No charge is made either for subsequent visits or for maternity care.*

ILWU/Warehousemen and Distributors Association Hospital and Medical Trust

ILWU Warehouse Locals 6 and 17 and the Distributors Association Hospital and Medical Trust also offer employees a choice of an indemnity plan underwritten by Pacific National and the Kaiser Foundation service plan. Employers pay the entire cost of health benefits for employees and dependents.

The indemnity plan provides both basic and major medical benefits with no differentiation between employee and dependents, except that the calendar year deductible under major medical is $200 for dependents and $100 for the employee.** Maximum hospital daily room and board reimbursement is $30 a day for 70 days, with all other charges paid in full. Top reimbursement for surgery is $1000. Physician visits are reimbursable at $5 per day in hospital, $5 at the office and $6 at home, up to $350 within six consecutive months for all illnesses and injuries.

Major medical insurance pays 80 percent after the deductible up to an overall maximum of $10,000 during any five consecutive years. Major medical, in addition

---

*See pp. 25-26 for fuller description of Kaiser plans.

**As in most contracts there is also a difference between employee and dependents in maternity benefits.

to the usual benefits, specifically provides reimbursement for outpatient prescribed medical supplies (including drugs) and for psychometric testing and psychotherapy performed outside the hospital at a top reimbursable fee of $20 per session for 50 sessions during a calendar year.

Eligible warehousemen may also choose the Kaiser plan, which offers the same benefits to employees and dependents. Benefits cover hospitalization, including board and room and all other hospital services, to 111 days for each illness or injury each year; physician's and surgeon's services, outpatient diagnostic tests, physical therapy, physical checkups and eye examinations, all at no charge except for physicians' home visits for which a charge is made only for the first two visits for each acute illness.

The ILWU Warehouse locals are also provided with a dental plan covering employees as well as dependents. This plan is underwritten by the Travelers Insurance Company of Hartford, Connecticut.

Northern California Retail Clerks/ Employers Welfare Fund

In the year 1968, this fund paid out more than $11 million for medical benefits on behalf of eligible retail clerks and their families. In addition, almost $331,000 were paid in benefits on behalf of retired employees and their spouses. Among persons covered by this fund are clerks working in retail stores, such as grocery, cigar, liquor, bakery, candy, and drug stores, furniture, shoe, jewelry, and men's specialty shops, department stores, women's specialty shops and variety stores. Employees covered by the fund may choose between an indemnity plan underwritten by the Union Labor Life Insurance Company and the Kaiser Foundation service plan.

All collectively bargained contracts provide for insured dental care. As contracts are renegotiated they also provide for comprehensive annual physical examinations for employees, for vision care and for prescription drugs for employees and dependents. Since April 1969, clauses covering retirees also include prescription drugs.

Employers pay 100 percent of the premium on behalf of employees but the employee pays for dependent coverage under a payroll deduction plan. Dependent benefits are similar to employee benefits.

There are two indemnity plans. Plan I provides somewhat higher benefits than Plan II, depending on the amount of employer contribution. The basic plan covers full reimbursement for hospital room and board in a three-or-more bed accommodation for either 70 days under Plan I or 120 days under Plan II and up to $1000 for other hospital charges. Surgical costs for any disability are reimbursed up to $1100 on the basis of the CMA relative value study. Reimbursement for physician visits is provided at the rate of $5 per day for office and home visits up to $400 per year and $4 per day for hospital visits for either 70 or 120 days (depending on entitlement). Licensed chiropractors, licensed chiropodists, and Christian Science practitioners are included in the term "doctor."

For out-of-hospital x-ray and laboratory services, Plan I pays $75 in each calendar year and Plan II pays $100 in each six-month period. In addition, Plan II pays the laboratory fee charged for routine Pap smears. Maternity benefits include both normal and abnormal delivery. Treatment of mental disorders is not specifically excluded from the basic plan.

If in any calendar year basic benefits paid by the plan or out-of-pocket expenses incurred by the employee (or both) exceed $200, a major medical benefit will pay 80 percent of the excess charges, if they are "usual, customary, and reasonable," up to $10,000. Plan II major medical covers treatment of mental illness in a hospital.

The Kaiser plan provides equal hospital, surgical and medical benefits for subscriber and dependents at no extra charge except for physician's first two home visits during each acute illness, and such items as outpatient drugs and injections, which are provided at "reasonable rates." No charge is made for 150 days' hospitalization each year (with 215 more days provided at health plan rates) or for maternity benefits.

This Kaiser plan allows up to 10 outpatient psychiatric visits at no charge, plus additional visits as required at $5 a visit. Referral by a doctor associated with the plan is not required. Up to 30 days' hospitalization for psychiatric conditions is provided each calendar year. Psychiatric conditions that in the opinion of Kaiser physicians cannot be improved through short-term therapy are excluded from coverage.

Dental care under the welfare fund is covered either by the California Dental Service, a free-choice plan, or by the Naismith Dental Group in their own offices.* Orthodontia, available only when specifically provided in the employer contract with the union, pays 50 percent of cost up to $500 per person.

Cost of vision care including glasses, for both employee and dependents, is reimbursed by the welfare fund when the employer has contributed to the fund for this purpose. Allowable each year are up to $22.50 for eye examinations, up to $25 for prescribed single-vision lenses and frames and $35 for bifocals. The Kaiser plan provides eye testing, refractions and therapeutic care when necessary as a regular medical benefit, but excludes eyeglasses.

A separate program covering 90 percent reimbursement of reasonable cost of prescription drugs is available under the welfare fund as this benefit is achieved at the bargaining table. Also available if prescribed by

---

*See pp. 28-29 for additional details on this provision.

a physician are self-injectables, dermatological preparations, special vitamins, diabetic supplies and miscellaneous items.

Northern California Teamsters Security Fund

Chief underwriters for the Teamsters Security Fund hospital and medical benefits are the Occidental Life Insurance Company of California and the Pacific National Life Assurance Company. Separate plans for the newer programs of vision and dental benefits are underwritten by the United Benefit Life Insurance Company of Omaha, Nebraska. Dual choice programs also offer service benefits under the Kaiser Foundation Health Plan.

Amount of reimbursement and extent of benefits under different indemnity plans vary from one segment of industry to another, but the fund trustees aim to negotiate improvements as plans come up for renewal. Coverage for all except.eligible seasonal workers is extended to dependents, although dependents' benefits may be limited to in-hospital treatment. Contracts for the most part provide major medical benefits in addition to the basic plan, with $100 deductible, 80 percent reimbursement and $10,000 maximum.

Basic plan benefits differ in detail. Payments toward hospital bills, for example, may be at the full charge in a three-bed ward for 70 days; at $28 per day for 20 days plus $38 for the next 50; $23 per day for 20 days plus $28 for the next 50; or $35 up to the maximum payable per disability. Maximum reimbursement per disability may be $1580 to $4000. Other hospital charges may be repaid in full or at a ceiling of $250. Reimbursement for surgical bills is made according to a fee schedule, with ceilings on total payment per disability ranging from $300 to $1000.

Similarly, reimbursement for physician's hospital or office visits may be set at $4 or $5 per day and home visits at $5 or $6 per day, with reimbursement covering the first visit for accidental injury but second or third visits for illness, and top total reimbursement for all physician visits set at $250, $300, or $350.

The Kaiser plan, where offered to Teamsters, provides 150 days' hospital services at no charge (plus 215 days at health plan rates), surgery, physicians' and specialists' office calls, physical therapy, diagnostic tests and radium therapy, maternity benefits, all at no charge for eligible employees and dependents.

The dental benefit, where applicable, covers both employee and dependents and pays 77 percent of the fee schedule or the actual charge, whichever is lower. The vision care benefit, where applicable, also covers both employee and dependents and provides vision testing once a year, one pair of lenses per year and frames once every two years. Reimbursement is the lower of either the actual charge or the amounts stated in a schedule of allowances. The maximum payable for frames is $8.

Oakland Restaurant and Tavern Welfare Fund

This fund covers about 5000 culinary workers, bartenders and cooks. Represented on the board of trustees are the Joint Board of Hotel and Restaurant Employees and Bartenders International Union, AFL-CIO, the East Bay Restaurant Association and the United Tavern Owners, Inc. Independent signatory employers also participate in the fund. The Oakland fund offers eligible employees either an indemnity plan underwritten by Occidental Life Insurance Company or a service plan under Kaiser.

The indemnity plan provides reimbursement for hospital room and board up to $48 per day in a three-bed ward for 70 days. Other hospital charges are reimbursed at 100 percent up to $500 and 75 percent of expenses in excess of that amount. Surgical costs, including anesthetist's charge, are reimbursed according to a fee schedule.

Physician's hospital visits are reimbursed at $5 a day up to $350. Hospital and surgical benefits are available both to members and dependents. Physician's home and office visits, available to members but not dependents, are reimbursed up to $375 a calendar year at a daily rate of $7.50 for home visits and $5 for office calls. Payment for any one accident begins on the first day of treatment but payment for any one illness begins only on the fourth day. The plan also provides a convalescent hospital benefit (following hospitalization).

The Kaiser plan negotiated by the Oakland fund provides equal benefits for eligible employees and their dependents. These cover 80 days' hospitalization and surgery at no charge, visits in doctor's or specialist's office at $1 per visit and out-of-hospital laboratory tests, x-ray and physical therapy at health plan rates.

The Oakland welfare fund also provides group dental insurance for eligible employees, underwritten by Occidental Life Insurance Company. Dependents are not covered. After a $20 deductible, insurance pays up to 75 percent of amounts designated in a fee schedule for restorative dentistry, oral surgery and replacement of natural teeth. No deductible is required for diagnostic and preventive dentistry, charges for which are also reimbursed up to 75 percent of the fee schedule.

San Francisco Culinary, Bartenders and Service Employees

Participating in the San Francisco Culinary, Bartenders and Service Employees Welfare Fund are:

Cooks' Union, Local 44; Bartenders' Union, Local 41; Waiters' Union, Local 30; Waitresses' Union, Local 48; Miscellaneous Culinary Employees' Union, Local 110; Hotel, Motel and Club Service Workers' Union, Local 283; and the Apartment, Motel, Hotel and Elevator Operators Employees' Union, Local 14, together with the Golden

Gate Restaurant Association, the Hotel Employers Association of San Francisco, the San Francisco Hotel Association, the San Francisco Club Institute and those employers not members of an association but parties to the agreements.

The health plan covers about 20,000 members for medical, surgical, hospital and prescription drug benefits. A dental benefit is being developed under a separate trust fund. The welfare fund pays the same monthly amount for each eligible member to either the Blue Shield or the Kaiser Foundation Health Plan, depending on the member's choice. The Kaiser premium covers both members and dependents.

Dependent coverage under Blue Shield, however, must be paid by the employee himself under a payroll deduction plan. Hospital and surgical benefits under Blue Shield are paid on an indemnity basis. Up to 50 physician home and office visits are included in service benefits when family income was $7500 or less in the year preceding service. Hospital benefits cover up to 100 days' care at a maximum rate of $33 per day, with a $300 ceiling on other hospital charges. Hospital and surgical benefits are available for both members and dependents, but doctor's home and office visits are covered for members only.

The Kaiser contract for eligible employees covers 111 days' hospitalization, surgery, unlimited doctor's office visits and other services, all at no charge. For dependents, the plan provides 60 days' hospitalization at no charge plus 50 days at health plan rates, surgical services at no charge, doctors' office visits at $1 per visit and other outpatient services at health plan rates.

A prescription drug benefit is available to all members of the San Francisco Culinary Welfare Fund, together with their eligible dependents. The Kaiser Foundation Health Plan partially covers prescription drugs, when such prescriptions are filled at a Kaiser Foundation pharmacy.

Culinary workers who choose Blue Shield coverage also receive substantial savings on prescription drugs upon presenting their identification cards to the Daylin Drug Stores, San Francisco. This arrangement is entirely independent of the Blue Shield contract, and payments are made directly to Daylin Drugs by the welfare fund.

San Francisco Lithographers Welfare Fund

The Printing Industries of Northern California and the Lithographers and Photoengravers International Union in a joint trust fund provide basic and major medical hospital, surgical, medical expense and vision benefits to eligible employees and their dependents. Dependents are defined to include unmarried children 19 to 23 years of age if they are students in an accredited institution. The underwriter for hospital and medical expense benefits is the Union Mutual Life Insurance Company; and for vision care, California Vision Services.*

Hospital benefits cover full charges in a three-bed ward for a maximum of 70 days, up to $1500 for other charges and $400 for surgery. The ceiling on physician office or home visits is $300 at $4 and $6 per day.

A major medical policy, with $100 deductible and a $10,000 maximum, pays 80 percent of charges and specifically includes payment for treatment of mental illness in a hospital at the same rates as for physical illness. Out-of-hospital treatment of mental illness is reimbursable at 50 percent, with $10 the maximum reimbursable per visit and a $500 maximum per year.

Sheet Metal Workers Welfare Plan of Northern California

The Sheet Metal Workers Welfare Plan of Northern California is administered by a board of trustees with

---

*See pp. 30-31 for details of vision benefits.

an equal number of employers and employee representatives. The plan is self-insured with payments made by the trustees from the trust fund, "only as funds are available therein for that purpose and to that extent only," according to the booklet issued to employees. The booklet goes on to say, "No other funds and no other person, firm, association, corporation, or other entity shall be liable for the payment of such benefits."

For both employees and dependents, the trust fund will reimburse $40 per day for hospital room and board up to 70 days and other hospital services to a maximum of $900; surgery in conformance with a fee schedule to $750; doctor's hospital visits at $5 per day up to $350 in any six-month period. The fund will pay up to $250 in any six-month period for office and home visits (at $5 and $6), except that for dependents, reimbursement is restricted to accidental injuries. For illness, maximum reimbursement is $100 a calendar year for *all* dependents. Outpatient surgery is allowed to $50 a year for both employee and dependent. A diagnostic x-ray and laboratory benefit pays up to $100 a calendar year not only for each accident or illness of the employee but for each accident and *all illnesses* of the dependent.

Provision is made for chiropractic at $3 per visit up to $50 a calendar year for both employees and dependents. X-ray and laboratory charges by the chiropractor are included in the maximum allowance.

A major medical provision covering employees pays 80 percent of expenses in excess of basic allowances, after a $100 deductible, up to $5000 for any one illness or accident. Hospitalization for mental illness is covered. Dependent coverage is limited to specified disabilities--polio, cancer or a malignant neoplasm.

The trust fund pays up to $25 for a routine physical examination each year for the employee and also provides him with vision care up to $50 a year.

United Steelworkers of America

An example of a nationwide agreement covering medical care is the United Steelworkers contract with steel corporations throughout the country. The program is administered by the employers through contracts with carriers mutually agreed upon by unions and management. Bay Area employers contract with Blue Cross and Blue Shield. Employers pay the full premium for basic services for eligible employees and dependents.

Blue Cross provides all hospital services in a semi-private room. Employees with less than 10 years' continuous service are covered up to 365 days for each hospitalization. Those with 10 or more years' continuous service at the beginning of a period of hospitalization are entitled to 730 days. When benefits are provided in connection with outpatient service, each visit to the outpatient department of a hospital counts as one day of hospitalization. (Benefits for hospitalization for a mental or nervous disorder are payable only up to 30 days in a 12-month period.) Provision is made for surgery, radiation therapy and diagnostic studies when performed in the outpatient department of a member hospital.

Blue Shield benefits for physicians' services cover surgery, obstetrics, in-hospital medical care, anesthesia, radiation therapy and diagnostic examinations either in or out of the hospital. Obstetrical services include prenatal and postnatal care. Full payment for services is made directly to the physician by Blue Shield on a prevailing fee basis.

Physicians' home and office visits are not covered.

A major medical plan reimburses 80 percent of specified medical expenses after a $50 deductible ($100 for a family) up to $10,000 in a calendar year and $20,000 in a lifetime. Physician office and home calls and prescription drugs are provided as well as other usual major medical benefits.

Also reimbursable are costs of treatment of mental and nervous conditions, for not more than $1000 in any calendar year. Therapy, individual and group, in physician's office or approved outpatient psychiatric facility is covered, as are professional services, other than a doctor's, through a day or night care program in an approved facility. In order to qualify as a covered medical expense, psychiatric services must be rendered for treatment of conditions that are amenable to favorable modification.

The collective bargaining agreement requires employers to furnish the union with an annual report regarding the health program.

CHAPTER *III*

Governmental Programs for Civilian Employees

The industry practice of sharing employees' medical care expenses is relatively new in governmental circles. Most of the civilian employees of federal, state and local governments in the Bay Area, however, now have available group health insurance plans, with the premiums partly paid by the employing agency.

FEDERAL EMPLOYEES

Federal government employees in the Bay Area may be covered by the health benefits program for federal employees that first became effective in July 1960. An employee may choose a governmentwide indemnity benefit plan administered on behalf of the insurance industry by the Aetna Life Insurance Company; a government service benefit plan administered by Blue Cross-Blue Shield; a number of employee organization plans; or prepaid group practice plans, such as Kaiser Foundation Health Plan. As of June 30, 1968, 52 percent of national enrollment was in the governmentwide service plan, 20 percent in the indemnity plan and the remainder in employee organization plans and prepaid group practice plans.

Employees may also choose between two levels of benefits. Close to 90 percent have chosen the higher level even though they alone bear the extra cost. Since January 1, 1971, the government pays 40 percent of the average premium for high-option coverage, whereas it formerly paid a fixed dollar contribution that amounted to about 24 percent of the premium for high-option family coverage. In no case may the government's contribution exceed 50 percent.[1]

Figures for coverage of federal employees in the Bay Area alone are not available, but the Civil Service Commission reports that as of June 1968, California enrollment in the health insurance program was 281,700 employees and annuitants, plus 532,700 dependents. More than one-fourth of these were covered by prepaid group practice plans.[2]

The largest of the governmentwide plans, the Blue Cross-Blue Shield Service Benefit Plan, provides 365 days of hospitalization under its high-option plan, and 30 days under the low option. Benefits for mental illness are now the same as those provided for other illnesses.

Out-of-hospital psychiatric care is covered at 80 percent of the charge (after a once-yearly $100 deductible) under the high-option plan, at 75 percent of the charge (with a $150 deductible) under the low option. Formerly insurance for psychiatric care was paid only at the 50 percent level. Blue Cross-Blue Shield covers day and night hospital care, group therapy, family therapy and services of a member of a "mental health team" (psychologist, psychiatric nurse or psychiatric social worker).

The Aetna Indemnity Benefit Plan reimburses 100 percent of the first $1000 hospital room and board charges for any type of illness, 80 percent of all other charges (75 percent under the low-option plan) and 80 percent of all other covered expenses after the first $1000. Early in 1967 the plan added coverage for day and night hospital care, group therapy, family therapy and services of a psychologist or psychiatric nurse when authorized by a psychiatrist. Until 1968, out-of-hospital psychiatric care was covered at 50 percent up to $250 a year, with a $50 deductible. Effective 1968, the coinsurance for out-of-hospital treatment was increased to 80 percent and the $250 per year limit was removed. The 1968 revisions also added coverage of social work service.

The Northern California Kaiser Foundation Health Plan provides up to 150 days' hospitalization at no charge (plus 215 days at health plan rates), unlimited office visits at $1 per visit and maternity care at $60 as well as the usual health plan services.*

In addition, federal employees are now provided with a psychiatric benefit at Kaiser facilities, bringing Kaiser into line with other federal employee insurers. The benefit covers outpatient treatment at $1 per visit for the first 10 visits and $5 each for all additional visits during a calendar year, plus prescribed psychological tests at health plan rates. Also covered are day care services at no charge up to 60 days each calendar year (minus two days for each day of hospitalization received during the year for psychiatric conditions) and prevailing rates thereafter. Full inpatient services, including hospital and professional services, are provided at no charge up to 30 days each calendar year (minus one day for each two days of day care received during the calendar year), and prevailing rates thereafter. All day care and most hospitalization for psychiatric conditions are provided at the Kaiser psychiatric center in Richmond.

Excluded is care for "chronic or organic psychiatric problems or conditions" which in the professional judgment of Kaiser plan doctors are not subject to significant improvement through short-term treatment.

CALIFORNIA STATE EMPLOYEES

California has contributed toward payment of the cost of employee health plans since January 1, 1962.

---

*See pp. 21 and 25-26 for a general description of Kaiser plans.

Persons employed by the state and working in state offices located in the Bay Area (including state colleges) are entitled to receive $10 a month toward the premium cost of an approved health plan.* Service and indemnity plans with high and low options are available to both active and retired employees. In the Bay Area, service plans include contracts with California Physicians Service (Blue Shield), Blue Cross, medical society foundations for medical care, and comprehensive group practice plans written by Kaiser Foundation Health Plan of Northern California.** There is one indemnity plan underwritten by the California-Western-Occidental insurance companies.

Total enrollment of California state and public agency employees, dependents and annuitants in health care plans was 114,000 in June 1969.[3] Membership was divided among the insurers as follows:

Type of plan	Percent of total
Service	37
Indemnity	31
Comprehensive group practice	30
Individual practice prepayment	2
County foundations for medical care	--
	100

The share of premium paid by the employing agencies amounted to 30 percent.

Approved health plans must provide at least the following benefits and be available to enrolled employees,

---

*As of August 1970. The state contribution was first $5, then $6 from October 1963, and $8 from November 1968 through July 1970.

**Statewide, also included are Kaiser Foundation Health Plan of Southern California, the Ross-Loos Plan (Los Angeles) and the Association of California State College Professors--Equity Educators Assurance Co., an indemnity plan.

annuitants and family members, including babies from birth: hospital--inpatient and outpatient; surgical, medical and diagnostic--in- and out-of-hospital; maternity and ambulance service benefits. Hospital benefits must be provided for the first 31 days of hospital confinement and include board and room as well as such charges as use of operating room and anesthetic supplies. All benefits must be sufficient to meet the major share of usual, customary and reasonable charges for such services.[4]

Indemnity Plan

Benefits for which charges are reimbursed by the Cal-Western-Occidental indemnity plan are summarized in the table below:

Benefits	Basic plan *Cal-Western-Occidental*
Hospital room and board	Up to $35 per day for first 70 days of hospitalization
Hospital services	Full payment of first $600 and 75 percent of next $1000 for first 70 days of hospitalization.
Surgical	Up to a maximum payment of $1000 per disability
Anesthetist	Benefits payable as a part of hospital services
Hospital diagnostic x-ray and laboratory	Benefits payable as a part of hospital services
Outpatient diagnostic x-ray and laboratory	Full payment up to first $150 per person per calendar year
Doctor's hospital calls*	Payment up to $6 per call (all members)

*Provides maximum of 50 calls per person per calendar year. A $20 per person annual deductible applies to home and office calls only.

Benefits (cont.)	Basic plan *Cal-Western-Occidental*
Doctor's office appointments*	Payment up to $5 per call (all members)
Doctor's house calls*	Payment up to $6 per call (all members)
Maternity	Hospital and medical benefits $175 for employee or annuitant, $125 for dependent spouse if pregnancy commences while insured

An optional major medical policy supplements this plan by reimbursement for additional hospitalization up to $50 a day; for 90 days in an extended care facility at no more than $10 a day; for hospitalization for mental illness; for speech therapy with a $1000 lifetime maximum; for rental of wheelchair, hospital bed and other equipment; for artificial limbs and eyes; and for outpatient drugs. These benefits are in addition to the usual reimbursement for medical expenses in excess of the reimbursement provided under the basic plan. Reimbursement is set at 80 percent after a general cash deductible of $100 and a special deductible of $50 for outpatient drugs, to a maximum of $40,000 for each disability.

Service Plans

The Blue Cross-Blue Shield service plan provides the following basic benefits:

Benefits	Basic plan *Blue Cross-Blue Shield*
Hospital room and board	Up to a three-or-more-bed ward rate for up to first 70 days of hospitalization

---

* See note on p. 71.

Benefits (cont.)	Basic plan *Blue Cross-Blue Shield*
Hospital services	Full payment during the first 70 days of hospitalization
Surgical	Payment in full
Anesthetist	Payment in full
Hospital diagnostic x-ray and laboratory	Full payment when hospitalized primarily for the treatment of an illness or injury
Outpatient diagnostic x-ray and laboratory	Up to a maximum payment of \$150 per person per calendar year
Doctor's hospital calls	Full payment during first 70 days of hospitalization for routine calls. Includes payment for approved consultations (all members)
Doctor's office and home calls	Full payment for accident and illness (employee only--no coverage for family members) (A \$25 deductible per person per calendar year applies for illness *only*.)
Maternity	Payment up to \$75 to the hospital; \$100 to the physician (employee or annuitant) Payment up to \$75 to the hospital; \$75 to the physician (dependent spouse) These benefits provided after nine months of membership

Hospitalization includes 30 days for treatment of mental illness in a Blue Cross contracting hospital or an allowance of \$12 a day in a noncontracting hospital. Benefits include psychiatric treatment while in the hospital.

A major medical policy underwritten by the California Physicians' Insurance Corporation includes reimbursement for expenses incurred in an extended care facility at $25 per day and $5000 lifetime maximum; speech therapy with a $5000 lifetime maximum; hospitalization for mental illness; and outpatient prescription drugs. The general cash deductible is $100 and the deductible for drugs is $50. Reimbursement is 80 percent of the first $15,000 and 100 percent of the next $25,000. The maximum for each disability is $40,000.

Principal Kaiser plan benefits for state employees are as follows:

Benefits	Basic plan *Kaiser North*
Hospital room and board	Up to 111 days each year each illness or injury, at no charge
Hospital services	No charge for the 111 days indicated above
Surgical	No charge
Anesthetist	No charge
Hospital diagnostic x-ray and laboratory	No charge
Outpatient diagnostic x-ray and laboratory	No charge
Doctor's hospital calls	No charge
Doctor's office calls	No charge--no limit
Doctor's home calls	Provided with $3.50 charge from 9 a.m. to 5 p.m. and $5 charge from 5 p.m. to 9 a.m. No charge after first two visits for acute illness
Maternity	All services provided with $60 charge. No waiting period
Out-of-area benefits	Up to $2000 per illness or injury provided while temporarily out of the area

The Kaiser plan also includes a partially prepaid outpatient prescription drug benefit.

A special major medical expense benefit for subscribers to the Kaiser Foundation Health Plan has been contracted for by the Public Employees' Retirement System, which administers the Meyers-Geddes State Employees Medical and Hospital Care Act. This plan, underwritten by the Cal-Western-Occidental companies, provides reimbursement at 80 percent of covered charges, after $100 deductible, up to $40,000 for any one disability.

Principal covered charges are:

1. Services and supplies for treatment of mental illness or functional mental disorder when confined in a hospital as a registered bed patient. The first $40 for each day of out-of-hospital psychiatric services of a physician are included.

2. Contagious diseases requiring isolation (excepting diagnostic services for such diseases), including tuberculosis, after the exhaustion of Kaiser Foundation Health Plan benefits.

3. Drugs or medicines bought while not confined in a hospital to the extent that they are not covered by Kaiser Foundation Health Plan's prepaid outpatient drug benefits, on a written prescription of a physician or surgeon contracting with the Kaiser Foundation Health Plan.

4. Corrective surgical and orthopedic appliances prescribed in writing by a physician or surgeon contracting with the Kaiser Foundation Health Plan in connection with an illness being treated by that physician.

5. Poliomyelitis either during the acute and contagious stages of the disease, or thereafter, for care and treatment received at a Rehabilitation Center of the Kaiser Foundation Health Plan or after the exhaustion of Kaiser Foundation Health Plan full post-polio benefits.

6. Medical care and services rendered by a Kaiser Foundation Health Plan Hospital or Kaiser Foundation Rehabilitation Center, drugs, medicines or private nursing care by a registered graduate nurse. These must be prescribed in writing by a physician or surgeon contracting with the Kaiser Foundation Health Plan, and are covered if charges are incurred during confinement as a registered bed patient after full coverage for hospitalization has been exhausted under the base plan in a contract year.

UNIVERSITY OF CALIFORNIA

Another statewide health insurance system in California is that provided for employees on all campuses of the University of California. This is similar to the state employee program except that the former is administered separately through the University. The Regents of the University contribute $10 per month toward the employee's insurance premium. In the Bay Area a choice of five different health plans is offered: two indemnity plans underwritten by the Equitable Life Assurance Society; and three service plans, one through the Kaiser Foundation Health Plan, one through Blue Cross-Blue Shield, and one, Blue Cross-Blue Shield plus a major medical indemnity plan.

The monthly contribution toward health care premiums in 1969, when the Regents' contribution was $8, was about 49 percent of actual cost for the employee and 19 percent for a family with two or more dependents (under the Equitable basic plus major medical plan). The equivalent percentages for Blue Cross-Blue Shield basic plus major medical was 56 percent and 20 percent, and for Kaiser 76 percent and 26 percent. Premiums for all plans were raised between 20 and 30 percent beginning January 1970, and some were further increased in April, further reducing the Regents' proportional share.

Indemnity Plan

The Equitable basic plan reimburses up to $35 or the three-bed ward rate, whichever is lower; up to 70 days for hospital board and room; in full up to $1950 for other hospital charges and up to $600 for surgery according to a fee schedule. Physician's hospital calls are allowed at $4 per day up to $280. Outpatient x-ray and laboratory tests are reimbursed according to schedule up to $100 per year for all illnesses and up to $100 per year for each accidental injury. There is no provision for physician's office or home visits.

Major medical under this plan pays 80 percent of excess costs over basic benefits (after the $100 annual deductible is met) up to $15,000. Major medical covers physician's office and home visits. It also pays for psychiatric care (excluded from basic benefits) up to 50 percent of inpatient and professional charges after deductible; out-of-hospital psychiatrist fees are reimbursed up to $10 per visit and $100 per calendar year, after deductible. A separate prescription drug benefit under major medical pays 80 percent of charges after a $50 deductible.

Dependents are entitled to the same benefits when premiums for their insurance are paid.

Service Plans

Blue Cross-Blue Shield. The basic service plan pays in full for hospital room and board and other services in a three-bed ward.* Unlimited physician's home and office calls are paid, for both illness and accidental injury for the subscriber only, after a $25 deductible

---

*As of January 1, 1971, Blue Cross assumed administration of the entire program, providing benefits formerly included under Blue Shield and California Physicians' Insurance Corp., as well as hospital benefits.

per calendar year. Dependents are covered only for accidental injury up to $100 a year. Outpatient x-ray and laboratory tests are covered up to $100 a year for each illness.

The basic plan also covers psychiatric care for 30 days in a member hospital, or pays $12 a day for 30 days in a nonmember hospital.

The combination Blue Cross-Blue Shield major medical plan covers the same basic services but costs in excess of basic benefits are reimbursed at 80 percent beyond the $100 deductible per calendar year. The 80 percent also applies to hospitalization for a psychiatric disorder; outpatient psychiatric care is reimbursed at 50 percent of cost, limited to $10 per visit and $100 per year.

Kaiser Foundation Health Plan. Coverage provides up to 150 days' hospital services at no charge (plus 215 additional days at health plan rates), as well as surgery and outpatient x-ray and laboratory tests at no charge. Doctor's office visits and routine physical examinations are provided at $1 per visit. Doctor's home visits cost $3.50 each visit ($5 evening) for the first two visits. There is a $60 charge for maternity care. Cost of emergency illness when out of the Kaiser service area is reimbursable up to $3000.

Prescriptions filled at a Kaiser pharmacy may be purchased by subscribers at half the wholesale price listed in the current price book for the smallest standard package, or $1, whichever is greater.

An in-hospital psychiatric benefit is provided up to a maximum value of $500 in each calendar year. If care is received at a Kaiser hospital, the subscriber receives treatment having a value of $1000 at health plan rates, and pays actual charges for additional care. If care is received in another institution, the member will be reimbursed up to $500. Effective January 1971, the University Regents have negotiated a major medical supplement to Kaiser Foundation Health Plans with the Equitable Life Assurance Society. After the $100 deductible, covered expenditures are reimbursed at 80 percent.

COUNTY GOVERNMENT EMPLOYEES

All nine Bay Area county governments sponsor group health care programs for their employees. Ninety percent of eligible employees are covered.

County Contribution

Four counties pay 100 percent of the employee premium; one pays 90 percent; one, 88 to 100 percent;* one, 47 percent; one, 40 percent; and one, 38 or 39 percent.** Only two counties pay a portion of the dependent premium, one at 9 percent and the other at 47 percent.

Insurance Underwriters

Seven counties offer employees a choice of two plans, either the Blues or Kaiser. One county offers a choice of four plans: (1) basic, system administered, plus major medical; (2) Kaiser; (3) Blue Shield plus major medical; (4) a small group panel plan, plus major medical. The one county that offers no choice to employees (but pays 100 percent of the health plan premium) sponsors a plan underwritten by an indemnity insurance company covering both basic and major medical benefits.

---

*Depending on which health plan the employee has chosen and on county agreement with different employee organizations.

**This is a flat $5 contribution; percentage depends on the cost of the plan selected.

In the 7 counties offering dual choice, the most popular plan is Kaiser in 3 counties, Blue Cross in 2 and Blue Shield in 1, and preference is evenly divided between Blue Cross and Kaiser in 1. Somewhat more than half the insured employees in the county sponsoring four plans have selected the system-administered program (listed as [1] above).

Program Benefits

The three Blues contracts differ in detail. One Blue Cross basic contract provides full payment of hospital charges for 100 days in a three-bed room with a $300 maximum on surgeon's charges, $3 for a doctor's hospital call for subscriber and dependent, and doctor's office and home calls at $3 and $4.50 to a maximum of $225 a year for the employee only. Major medical in this contract specifically covers prescription drugs at 80 percent after deductible.

The second basic Blue Cross contract provides full cost of hospitalization in a three-bed ward for 31 days with $1000 limit on surgery (plus $1000 for radium therapy) and no outpatient physician services for either subscriber or dependent. The major medical in this contract covers limited reimbursement for hospital care of mental illness and also covers prescription drugs.

The Blue Shield contract provides full payment for 100 days of hospital room and board in a three-bed room, with a $500 ceiling on other hospital charges, and surgeon's services based on a fee schedule. Provision is made for limited coverage of both hospital and outpatient psychiatric services.

In the counties where most employees chose the Kaiser plan, two were of the "U" type and one "J."* The "U" plans provided 150 days' hospital coverage at no

---

*For Kaiser plans, see also p. 84.

charge (plus 215 days at health plan rates), unlimited physician office visits at $1 per visit and a $60 maternity care charge. The "J" plan differed chiefly in that there was no extra charge for office visits or for maternity care.

The system-administered basic plan in the county offering a choice of four plans provided 31 days' hospitalization at $50 a day plus a maximum of $500 for other hospital charges, surgical benefits based on a fee schedule, physician's office and home visits to $275 a year (with the cost of the first two visits for illness not covered). Major medical covered 80 percent of medical expenses in excess of the basic plan (after $75 deductible) to a $20,000 lifetime limit. Outpatient prescription drugs and limited psychiatric care were included.

The indemnity insurance contract sponsored by another county provided reimbursement for 180 days' hospital room and board, for surgical benefits based on a fee schedule to $1100 for physician's hospital and office visits at $6 per visit, and for limited hospital treatment of mental illness. Major medical maximum reimbursement was $20,000 and included coverage of prescription drugs.

Supplemental Plans

No county sponsored supplemental plans for group coverage of dental or vision care or for prescription drugs.

CITY GOVERNMENTS

Three out of every 4 Bay Area cities with populations of 5000 or more replied to the Institute of Governmental Studies questionnaire on health insurance. Only 2 percent of the respondents reported that they had no group insurance for employees, indicating that 93 percent of more than 18,000 salaried employees are covered by city-sponsored plans.*

Full cost of the premium for salaried employees was paid by 83 percent of the cities with health plans, and part was paid by 15 percent. No contribution was made by 2 percent of the responding cities. One out of every 10 cities paid the full premium for at least one dependent in addition to the employee's premium and 2 out of 10 paid part of the dependent's premium.** No part of the dependent premium was paid by 7 out of 10 city governments.***

Where alternate health plans were offered employees, selection in 6 of every 10 cities was evenly divided between the Kaiser plan and the Blues. Where no choice was offered, however, two-thirds of the plans were underwritten by the Blues, and most of the others by indemnity insurance companies.

Indemnity Plans

Terms of the indemnity insurance policies varied greatly. Basic plan reimbursement for hospital room and board ran from $25 to $45 a day for 70 or 90 days and the maximum on other hospital charges ranged from $300 to $500. Reimbursement for surgery was based on a fee schedule with ceilings from $300 to $900. Doctors' office and home visits were reimbursed at $4 and $5 per visit.

---

*Not all employees chose to be covered by city plans.

**No information was given for hourly employees, if any. Where such employees work under union contracts, the city contribution to premiums varies according to contract.

***It must be pointed out that in a recent election taxpayers in one large city overwhelmingly defeated a proposition that would have permitted the city to pay full costs of employee membership in a health care plan.

Blue Cross-Blue Shield

All but a minor percentage of Blue plans provided major medical as well as basic benefits. Hospitalization was provided at full cost for 100 days in 55 percent of the basic plans, for 70 days in 24 percent, for 31 days in 7 percent, and for 21 days in 14 percent. Other hospital charges were paid in full, and surgeons' fees were based on a fee schedule in virtually all Blue Cross plans.

Doctors' home visits and office appointments were available only under major medical in almost 3 out of 4 Blue contracts. Where they were covered, office visits were payable at $5 and $6 and house calls from $5 to $10, with calendar-year ceilings ranging from $225 to $420.

Some hospital care for mental illness was provided in 7 out of every 10 basic plans. In almost half of these plans, major medical made limited reimbursement for outpatient psychiatric care.

Kaiser Foundation

In cities where most of the employees had chosen enrollment in the Kaiser plan, 4 out of 10 plans were of the "U" type, 3 out of 10 were "J," 2 were "B" and 1 was "D." The chief differences in these plans relate to hospital benefits, payment for physician visits and for maternity care. "U" and "J" coverage provide 150 days' hospitalization (plus 215 at health plan rates) and "B" and "D," 111 days. Office visits are provided at no charge by "J" and "D." In addition, the "C" plan charges health plan rates for both in-hospital and out-of-hospital x-ray and laboratory tests, x-ray therapy, and physical therapy. The Kaiser plans provided outpatient drugs at "reasonable rates." Their principal differences are as follows:

Plan	Days' hospitalization	Charge for office visits	Charge for maternity care
J	150, 215[a]	No charge	No charge
B	111	$1	$60, $140[b]
U	150, 215[a]	$1	$60
D	111	No charge	No charge
C	60, 51[a]	$1	$95, $140[b]

[a]Additional days billed at health plan rates.

[b]If confinement due before 10 months' membership.

SCHOOL DISTRICT EMPLOYEES

Two-thirds of the 245 school districts in the Bay Area include elementary grades only. Twelve percent are high school or junior high school districts and 5 percent, junior college districts. Unified districts comprise 17 percent of the total.

Although school districts, like many other governmental agencies, have lagged behind industry in providing access to group insurance, there now appears to be a growing recognition of the value of hospital and medical insurance as a major fringe benefit for both certificated and classified employees. The state laws permit school districts to provide for group health insurance, and authorize an override tax to pay the district costs.[5]

Employer Contribution

Two out of every 3 school district respondents reported paying the full premium for employee health care coverage in 1969. With few exceptions, the other districts made some contribution to the cost of employee coverage, usually a fixed dollar amount.* The entire

*In a number of districts that contributed a fixed monthly amount to the premium, the amount at one time paid nearly the entire premium for the employee, but rising rates reduced the proportion of the contribution.

premium for both employee and dependent was paid in 2 out of every 10 districts, and partially paid in 1 out of every 10. Seven out of 10 districts for which this information was available made no contribution toward dependent coverage.

Choice of Plan

On the basis of information from 189 school districts including grades 1-14, it is estimated that 3 out of every 4 districts with health care plans offer employees a choice between Blue Cross plus major medical or the Kaiser Foundation Health Plan. Blue Cross was far the more popular in part, perhaps, because these plans were negotiated on the basis of California Teachers Association purchasing power. In all but a few cases where no choice was offered, moreover, the underwriter was Blue Cross. Where there was a choice, the majority of employees selected Blue Cross over Kaiser in half the school district plans reported, whereas a majority chose Kaiser in only 20 percent. Choice was evenly divided between the two in 30 percent of the reporting districts.

Commercial insurance contracts, limited to major medical coverage, were the sole plans available to employees in 4 percent of the reporting districts.*

Blue Cross Plans

Although the Blue Cross plans reviewed for this study differed in a number of benefits offered, all basic coverage assured full payment directly to providers of certain services. Hospitalization covered either 180 or 365 days' room and board in a three-bed room, as well as full payment for all other usual hospital

---

*The district paid for the full premium for the employee but not for his dependents.

charges. Payment to surgeons and other specialists was made according to a fee schedule based on the CMA relative value study or, more commonly, on the basis of "usual, customary, and reasonable charges." Payments for physician's hospital visits ranged from $3 to $15 a day and were frequently made on the basis of customary and reasonable charges.

Five out of every 6 contracts also provided for care in a convalescent facility after at least five days in a hospital. Blue Cross paid in full in a contracting facility, or up to $20 a day in a noncontracting facility. Each day of care reduced allowed hospital days by one-half day. Major medical covered charges exceeding the basic benefit in 3 out of every 5 contracts providing convalescent care.

Basic Blue Cross coverage excluded hospitalization occurring primarily for diagnostic tests, medical observation, physiotherapy and hydrotherapy. In the plans reviewed, this benefit was available under major medical in 9 out of every 10 plans, with the usual deductible and copayment.*

Other benefits. Doctor's home and office visits were provided under basic coverage for both subscriber and dependents in 62 percent of the contracts, for the subscriber alone in 23 percent, and not at all in 15 percent. Where out-of-hospital visits were provided for both, fees were fixed at $6 for office visits and $9 for house calls to an overall total of $420 a year. Where the benefit was for the subscriber only, fees were $3, $4, $5 for office visits and $4.50, $6 and $7 for house calls, with a maximum payment of $225, $300 or $350 for the two. Major medical covered out-of-hospital physician visits where this benefit was not included in the basic plan.

All but 15 percent of the plans examined provided for outpatient diagnostic studies for both subscribers

---

*Only 5 percent of the Blue Cross plans did not include major medical coverage.

and dependents to a maximum of $150. Basic coverage also provided an additional accident benefit, x-ray therapy, ambulance service, and some maternity benefits for both subscribers and dependents. It specifically excluded routine physical examinations, dental care (except as a result of an accident when hospitalized), eye refractions, eyeglasses and outpatient prescribed drugs.

Psychiatric care. A benefit seldom found in commercial basic contracts or the Kaiser plans provides 30 days a year in a contracting hospital for care of mental disorders at full cost, or $12 a day in a noncontracting hospital with major medical picking up 80 percent of the charges in excess of the basic plan benefit. This benefit was included in 85 percent of the plans reviewed. It was provided only under major medical in an additional 10 percent, and omitted in only 5 percent.

Major medical also covered outpatient psychiatric care in 3 out of every 4 plans reviewed, paying 50 percent of the fee to $15 for each visit (that is, $7.50) after deductible, with a maximum of 50 visits each calendar year. According to the California Teachers Association, all its Blue Cross major medical contracts include outpatient psychiatric care since July 1, 1969.

Blue Cross major medical. The most common deductible in the major medical plans reviewed was $50 per calendar year, although 1 out of every 5 carried a $100 deductible. Ordinarily only three deductibles were necessary for one family. The maximum lifetime reimbursement of $20,000 for all benefits was raised to $50,000 as of July 1, 1969, according to the California Teachers Association, with $1000 automatically restored each January 1. Major medical reimbursement was based on the usual, customary and reasonable charges of the area in which the member received service.

Major medical benefits, besides those already mentioned, included provision for outpatient prescribed drugs, special nursing, artificial limbs, blood transfusions, mechanical equipment and cosmetic surgery, all at 80 percent of cost after deductible.

Kaiser Plans

In school districts where the majority of employees had subscribed to the Kaiser plan (20 percent of those reporting), 3 out of every 4 contracts were in the "J" category. Under this plan, school district employees and their dependents were provided with 150 days' hospitalization for each illness annually at no charge, plus 215 days at health care rates, physicians' office visits and maternity care at no charge and partially prepaid prescription drugs.

The remaining contracts were either in the "U" or "B" category. "U" coverage is similar to "J" except that a charge of $1 is made for each office visit and $60 for maternity care. "B" coverage provides 111 days' hospitalization, with charges for office visits and maternity care the same as under "U" coverage.

One Kaiser contract provided psychiatric care at reduced rates.

Supplemental Services

Twenty percent of the school districts sponsored prepaid dental insurance, chiefly for the employee only, under a separate policy.* Four percent sponsored a

---

*Property taxpayers are not always in favor of fringe benefits for school employees, as witness a letter to the editor of a local newspaper: "Sir: I wonder how many of the residents in the...school district realize that their taxes will be increased this year because they have to pay for the dental insurance of all...school district employees. All will be covered and the district will pay the entire premium. The taxpayers have nothing to say about this new tax, and, resentfully, are forced to pay it. Now when you see a...school district employee flashing a toothy smile, just remember you're helping to pay for it."

separate policy covering prepaid prescribed drugs. Less than one-half of 1 percent offered a separate policy for vision care.

CHAPTER *IV*

Special Population Groups

Many Bay Area residents are eligible for free or part-paid medical care under programs for which the federal government has assumed primary responsibility. Federal agencies either provide care in government facilities or purchase it on behalf of these beneficiaries. Members of the uniformed services--army, navy, air force, marine corps, coast guard, commissioned corps of the public health service--and their families, merchant seamen and eligible veterans of the armed services are entitled to such care.

The federal government is also responsible for the national program of health insurance for the aged: Medicare. In addition it pays the major cost of state programs of medical aid (Medicaid) for persons eligible for federal-state programs of public assistance and certain medically needy persons. In California, this program is known as Medi-Cal. County governments have responsibility, under California law, for medical care of needy persons who are not eligible for state aid.

MEMBERS OF ARMED FORCES

A comprehensive medical care system provides direct service for active members of the armed forces. The government sets up facilities and hires professional personnel. Dependents of active-duty personnel are also entitled to medical care under this system. Dependents include spouse, unmarried legitimate children, adopted children and stepchildren under age 21 or older if attending school or college; it also includes those who are dependent because of mental or physical disability. Covered care includes hospitalization, surgery, acute medical care, obstetrical and maternity care, treatment of acute emotional disorders, pre- and post-hospital diagnostic procedures and treatment of injuries on an outpatient basis.

Since December 1956 dependents have been able to choose between military and civilian facilities for in-hospital care, including obstetrical and maternity care. Payments to providers of service are made through Blue Shield and Blue Cross and also Mutual of Omaha, an indemnity insurance company. Outpatient services are provided through military hospitals and clinics. Providers of care are reimbursed on the basis of a fee schedule negotiated annually. Excluded from private treatment are outpatient care of mental and nervous disorders, care of chronic disease, elective medical and surgical treatment and dental care. In 1969-70 Defense Department expenditures for all medical care amounted to $1.9 billion.[1]

MERCHANT SEAMEN

Members of the U.S. merchant marine are entitled to medical care without charge at hospitals maintained by the U.S. Public Health Service.* The federal government has assumed responsibility for direct services to merchant seamen ever since 1798 when the Congress provided for compulsory deductions from the wages of seamen for their hospital care. The Public Health Service hospital in San Francisco provides both outpatient and hospital care for merchant seamen in the Bay Area. Dependents of persons in the U.S. armed services and U.S. government employees injured on the job are also eligible for service at the hospital.

---

*Public Health Service also provides direct services for American Indians, primarily those living on reservations.

VETERANS

Since 1919, veterans of the armed services have received hospital and outpatient care when needed as a result of service-connected medical or compensable dental conditions. Treatment is at Veterans Administration hospitals or clinics, or the VA may pay for outpatient care by a "hometown" doctor or dentist if prior approval is obtained.

VA hospital care may be given on a bed-available basis for treatment of nonservice-connected conditions, provided the veteran claims inability to defray costs of such care.* Outpatient ambulatory care is sometimes also provided for nonservice-connected conditions when it is apparent that length of hospital stay is being prolonged because of inability to receive outpatient care.

Total VA expenditures for hospital and medical care in fiscal 1970 were $1.6 billion.[2]

Federal responsibility for medical care of veterans of the armed forces has become of increasing importance as a consequence of the expanding numbers who have served in the armed forces.

THE AGED, MEDICARE AND ITS SUPPLEMENT

About 395,000 individuals in the Bay Area are eligible to receive hospital and related benefits under

---

*An applicant is required to fill out a financial statement. If review of the statement suggests the applicant can afford private care, he is so informed. If he nevertheless insists on VA treatment, he is given the benefit of the doubt, and the statement is referred to VA attorneys for possible recovery of costs. In 1970, Congress exempted veterans over age 65 from this procedure, on the basis that care in a VA hospital was less costly than payments to private hospitals under Medicare.

the federal program of Health Insurance for the Aged, known as Medicare. Almost that many are eligible for physicians' services under a voluntary supplementary program. The program was enacted by Congress in 1965 after many years of unmitigated opposition by organized medicine.[3] The law went into effect July 1, 1966.

Health insurance for the aged, Title XVIII of the Social Security Act, in many respects resembles private insurance but is financed in part by the federal treasury. The law provides a mechanism for paying for medical care but does not guarantee its availability or its quality. Both hospital insurance and medical insurance claims for reimbursement for services rendered are handled through fiscal intermediaries--commercial insurance companies or carriers like Blue Cross and Blue Shield--which are paid for their costs of administration.* In northern California, Blue Shield and Blue Cross are the fiscal intermediaries for Medicare. Providers of hospital and medical services are paid on the basis of "reasonable" cost or charge.

Total public expenditures for the Medicare program in fiscal 1969-70 were $7.1 billion.[4] In 1968-69 the program paid 47 percent of the total personal health care expenditures of the aged, meeting 66 percent of their hospital bills and 72 percent of their physicians' bills.[5]

Cost to Beneficiary

Hospital and related benefits under Part A of the program are paid through an additional Social Security tax on earnings up to $7800, amounting in 1970 to 0.6 of 1 percent applied equally to employees, employers and self-employed, and scheduled (as of 1970) to rise gradually to 0.9 percent by 1987. Starting in January

---

*Under hospital insurance, however, any provider of service is free to deal directly with the government.

1971 beneficiaries must pay a deductible of $60 for the first 60 days' hospitalization (up from the 1966 deductible of $40), with the remaining cost paid by Medicare. Beneficiaries also pay $15 a day for the 61st through 90th day of hospitalization and $30 a day for every day used in a so-called "lifetime reserve" of 60 days. A deductible of $7.50 a day is also charged in an extended care facility for the 21st through the 100th day.*

Supplementary medical insurance, a voluntary program under Part B, helps pay for physicians' and related services. The premium for those choosing these benefits is $5.30 a month, which is to be raised to $5.60 beginning July 1, 1971, a 40 percent increase over the $4 premium in force from April 1968 to July 1970, and 87 percent higher than the original $3 premium. An equal amount per beneficiary per month is paid by the federal government.

After a $50 deductible each year, the beneficiary is reimbursed 80 percent of the "reasonable" fee for covered expenses. Nothing in the law (as of March 1971) prevents a physician from charging what he wishes above the reimbursable amount.**

---

*These deductibles are 15 percent higher than they were in 1970, and 50 percent higher than when Medicare went into effect.

**It was originally supposed that medical insurance would provide a service benefit, with the physician or other supplier billing the government through the insurance intermediary. Most doctors, however, seem to prefer billing the patient directly. The beneficiary may pay the bill, put in a claim and wait interminably for reimbursement. He may finally get much less than 80 percent of his claim, moreover, because his doctor's fee was not "reasonable." This presents an added burden on the lower income aged.

Hospital Benefits--Part A

Coverage during one benefit period includes up to 90 days in a hospital, plus all services ordinarily furnished by a hospital to its patients, and up to 100 days in an extended care facility after at least three days in a hospital. An extended care facility is defined as one primarily engaged in providing skilled nursing and rehabilitation services to inpatients. In addition, each beneficiary is entitled to a lifetime reserve of an additional 60 hospital days.

Care in a psychiatric hospital is covered only if the physician certifies that treatment can "reasonably be expected to improve" the patient's condition. It is limited to 190 days in the beneficiary's lifetime.

After the patient's hospitalization or stay in an extended care facility, the program pays for specified home health services for up to 100 days in one year. Home health services include intermittent or part-time nursing care, physical, occupational, or speech therapy, medical social services, part-time health aide (*not* a homemaker or household helper), medical supplies and use of medical appliances. Each service furnished during a day counts as one "visit." Services must be supplied by a qualified home health agency under a plan established and reviewed periodically by the patient's physician.

Medical Insurance Benefits--Part B

The following benefits are provided under medical insurance: physicians' and surgeons' services, whereever furnished; diagnostic tests; x-ray, radium, and radioactive isotope therapy; ambulance service; also, such supplies as surgical dressings, splints and casts; medical equipment such as iron lungs, oxygen tents, hospital beds, and wheelchairs used in the patient's home; prosthetic devices such as braces and artificial legs, arms and eyes; and home health services, as defined in the basic hospital plan, with no requirement of prior hospitalization, for up to 100 visits during each calendar year.

A special limitation is placed on benefits for out-of-hospital treatment of mental, psychoneurotic and personality disorders. During a calendar year the maximum amount reimbursable under the plan (after the usual deductible) is $312.50 or 62.5 percent of the expense, whichever is smaller. Since only 80 percent of incurred expenses can be paid, the ceiling, in effect, is $250 or 50 percent.

THE IMPOVERISHED

Divers fragmented services exist to meet medical needs of people unable to pay in full for their care. Chief among these services are the publicly supported programs intended for the care of aged, blind and disabled people and poor families with dependent children who meet welfare eligibility standards. The U.S. Social and Rehabilitation Service pays 50 to 83 percent of the cost of such care.

Other health care programs, heavily supported by the U.S. Children's Bureau, now a unit of the Public Health Service, are financed for specific periods on a "pilot project" basis. Among them are maternal and infant care, children's and youth care and family planning programs. Several operate in San Francisco, Berkeley and Oakland, including one at the Mount Zion Hospital medical center, which provides direct services to children in San Francisco's Western Addition. Crippled Children's Services also operate with Public Health funds. Federal moneys also support such programs as neighborhood health centers that offer health care services in poverty or near-poverty areas.

On the local level, California county health departments may provide free or part-pay screening and preventive services but rarely treatment, with patients being referred to private doctors or the county hospitals. Public health clinics may provide screening for cancer, diabetes, tuberculosis and venereal disease. Preventive services may include immunization, prenatal and well-child care and family planning as well as health education.

In addition, there exist privately supported so-called "free clinics" for special groups, usually operating with insufficient funds and with voluntary staff on a part-time basis. Examples of these are Berkeley's Free Clinic, the Haight-Ashbury Free Clinic and the Fillmore Black Man's Free Store Clinic. To discuss in detail the relationship of all these programs to medically needy Bay Area residents is too great a task for this monograph. The following sections are limited to a description of the federal-state program for persons eligible for public assistance, the neighborhood health centers and the role of the county hospitals.

MEDICAID AND MEDI-CAL

Until October 1, 1957, when Public Assistance Medical Care (PAMC) was established as a federally subsidized statewide program for outpatient care for specified groups of welfare recipients, California county boards of supervisors had prime responsibility for medical care of all needy residents. In 1960 another federal program, Medical Assistance for the Aged (MAA), enabled the state to provide hospital and nursing home care and some outpatient services for medically indigent aged as well as inpatient services for recipients of old age assistance.

Both PAMC and MAA were absorbed into the statewide 1966 program, Medi-Cal, enacted under the spur of Title XIX of the Social Security Act.

Title XIX, known as Medicaid, aimed to substitute a single system of medical assistance for the many existing fragmented services administered through the federal-state welfare programs. It was designed to encourage the states, through more liberal subsidization by the federal government, to provide improved medical care not only for recipients of federal-state welfare aid but also for medically needy persons who could pay their day-to-day living expenses but needed help to pay medical bills.[6] To attain this end, Title XIX provided that federal funds would be paid only to states that made a satisfactory effort toward broadening their existing medical care programs, "with a view toward furnishing by July 1, 1975, comprehensive care and services to substantially all individuals who meet the plan's eligibility standards with respect to income and resources."[7] In fiscal 1969-70, the total spent on Medicaid was more than $5 billion, of which the federal government spent more than half.[8]

Medi-Cal is the California Medicaid program.* Total cost of the program in 1968-69 amounted to $754.8 million. Beneficiaries under Medi-Cal have free choice of physician and medical facility. All payments to hospitals, physicians and other providers of service are made through the "fiscal intermediaries," Blue Shield and Blue Cross. In the past, payments to doctors have been made on the basis of "usual and customary fees" and to other providers according to a maximum fee schedule set by the State Department of Finance. Hospitals have been paid on the basis of "reasonable costs."

---

*Medi-Cal was authorized by the 1965 Legislature after debate that continued through eight months and three legislative sessions. Participating in writing the program were the California Medical Association (CMA), the California Hospital Association, and other professional associations of providers of service, as well as the County Supervisors Association of California, together with state officials and members of the Legislature. Organized labor endorsed it, and it had bipartisan support. The Legislature stipulated that as soon as feasible, the program was to be converted into a system of prepaid health insurance, thus eliminating the stigma of charity care.

Persons Eligible

Medi-Cal is open to two groups of residents: Group 1 denotes persons eligible for cash grants under the federally subsidized public assistance programs; and Group 2, so-called "medically needy" persons. In Group 1 are persons receiving cash grants under old age assistance, aid to the blind, aid to the disabled and aid to families with dependent children (AFDC).* Persons or families who qualify for these programs but do not wish to apply for cash aid are also eligible. Children in foster care whose needs are met in whole or in part from public funds are also entitled to medical benefits, as are all children under age 21 in families receiving children's aid.

Group 2 covers people who are in all respects similar to the first group except that they have sufficient resources to pay their day-to-day living expenses but not enough to pay all medical bills. They are classified as medically needy and are either old, blind or disabled or meet the requirements for aid to families with dependent children.**

---

*Besides being in financial need, children are eligible for AFDC only if they are deprived of the support of one or both parents because of illness, death or separation. Unemployment was recently added as a cause of deprivation. To receive federal aid, the children must be living with specified relatives. Children between the ages of 18 and 21 are not eligible for cash assistance unless they are attending school or participating in a training program. Children in intact families where the parent is employed, no matter how low the wages, are not eligible for federal-state aid, either for maintenance or medical care.

**Requirements include the obligation for a mother seeking help for her children--whether for maintenance or medical care--to cooperate with the district attorney in locating their absent father. Also, to receive any aid at all, family adults with employment potential must accept referral to the State Division of Vocational Rehabilitation for job training or retraining.

About 122,555 aged, blind and disabled poor persons in the Bay Area were eligible for the program in June 1970. Almost 18 percent of them were in the medically needy group, that is, they needed public aid only in paying their medical bills. In addition, 90,246 families with 214,450 children were potential beneficiaries of the program. Ten percent of the families were in the medically needy category.[9] Also eligible for medical assistance as of June 1970 were 9406 children in boarding homes, of whom 20 percent were medically needy only.

Patients' Share of Cost

Group 1 beneficiaries are entitled to benefits at no cost except for persons in long-term care institutions and with incomes of more than $15 a month. They are required to share in the cost, usually from their public assistance grants or from their Social Security benefits.

Group 2 benefits are available to eligible persons only after all their income and resources in excess of their maintenance needs has been used to pay their medical liabilities. About 50,000 medically needy persons were dropped from the Medi-Cal rolls in July 1970 through further restrictions on allowable resources and a reduction in the amount of maintenance need.

Maintenance Need

Maintenance need is the sum allocated to the living expenses of the household. Beginning August 1, 1970, total maintenance need was reduced to $158 a month for a single individual; to $200 for a two-person family; $233 for a three-person family; and $300 for a family of four.* The maintenance standard for families of five

---

*These amounts constitute the maximum allowed for maintenance for families of this size if federal sharing in the cost of their medical care is to be obtained. They are a great deal lower than the amounts originally permitted for maintenance need. As of September 1967, for

or more persons ranges from $358 for five, to $517 for 10 in one family (plus $8 per month for each additional person).[10]

Reserves

California law allows a personal property reserve of $1200 for a single person, with a $100 increment for each additional person in the family up to a maximum of $2000 for a family of nine or more. A home used as a residence is exempt from consideration as a resource. Ownership of other real property assessed at more than $5000 disqualifies an applicant for benefits. Ownership of real property assessed below that sum is allowed, but a monthly income value is set on it amounting to (1) the actual net income or (2) 1/12 of 6 percent of the market value, whichever is greater. (Principal payments on the property are not deducted in determining net income.)[11]

Benefits Available

Since August 1, 1970 both Group 1 and Group 2 beneficiaries are entitled to an equal range of benefits under the law. These are inpatient and outpatient hospital services; physicians' services in office, home, hospital, nursing home or elsewhere; skilled nursing home care; laboratory, x-ray and radiology services and

---

example, maintenance need for one person was judged to be $173 a month; for two, $289; and for four, $341. Under the 1967 Social Security amendments, the federal government does not share in state expenditures for medical services rendered to medically needy persons for whom the state plan allows a maintenance standard more than a third above that allowed by state assistance payments to families of the same size who are on aid to families with dependent children. AFDC allowances in California have been much lower than those for the aged, blind or disabled.

home health care services.* In addition, the original program provided approved drugs and medical supplies; dental services; optometric services; hearing aids prescribed by physicians; services of physical, occupational or speech therapists, audiologists, and psychologists; eyeglasses, artificial eyes and other eye appliances; prosthetic and orthopedic devices--braces, crutches, artificial limbs; prescribed medical equipment; medical transportation such as "Servi-Car" and "Handi-Cab"; inpatient and outpatient rehabilitation center services; blood and blood substitutes; podiatry services, other than routine care of the feet; chiropractic services; other legally recognized medical services such as Christian Science practitioners and faith healers.**

Before August 1, 1970 a Group 2 beneficiary (the medically needy person not receiving welfare) could receive the above additional benefits only when he was a patient in a hospital or nursing home and the benefit was prescribed by his physician. If the benefit was related to the medical problem for which he was institutionalized and was prescribed by his physician, it was also available as a program benefit during 90 days after discharge from hospital or nursing home.

Many of the services listed required prior authorization by a Medi-Cal consultant if they exceeded a specified number of visits within a specified period, or cost above a specified sum.

---

*For persons 65 and over, Medi-Cal benefits supplement those available under Medicare. Since January 1, 1970 Medi-Cal can pay the premium and other Medicare out-of-pocket costs for eligible medically needy persons. This benefit was previously available only for persons eligible for cash grants in the aged, blind or disabled programs.

**Most of these additional benefits are not covered under basic insurance policies written for the general public, but some are being written into major medical policies. People whose incomes are well above the poverty level may purchase such services individually for themselves and their dependents.

Most of the Medi-Cal benefits except hospitalization were available to recipients of old age assistance, aid to the blind and aid to the disabled, and to medically needy aged persons under the former state PAMC and MAA programs (Public Assistance Medical Care and Medical Assistance for the Aged). Some services were also available to eligible children in families with dependent children. Medi-Cal extended equal services to eligible adults in the dependent children's program in accordance with federal requirements.

Financial Crisis

For the third time since it began, Medi-Cal faced a financial crisis in 1970.[12] Projected budget shortages arising out of an anticipated increase in the public assistance rolls gave rise to drastic changes in the program early in December 1970.[13] Virtually all services were placed on an emergency-only basis, and payments to all providers, except hospitals, were cut by 10 percent.* A new drug formulary was issued with tightened restrictions on the use of many items without prior authorization from a Medi-Cal consultant.

Emergency services were defined as those "rendered under unforeseen conditions which require hospitalization, or admission to a nursing home or convalescent home, or services for the repair of accidental injury, relief of acute pain, elimination of acute infection, protection of the public health, or the amelioration of illness, which if not immediately diagnosed and treated would lead to disability or death..."

All except such emergency services were designated "elective" and required prior authorization by a Medi-Cal

---

*Federal requirements mandate reimbursement for reasonable costs of inpatient hospital care.

consultant.* Medi-Cal consultants were instructed that "any service authorized must be one that cannot be postponed for 90 days or more without seriously affecting the health of the beneficiary.**

Prior authorization was required, for example, for more than two physicians' office visits or home calls per month (except for emergency), for more than one psychiatric service or more than one dental visit in six months and for all nonemergency optometric services including eye refractions.

Widespread protest against the cuts materialized at once. Witnesses at hearings held by the Assembly Public Health Committee called the cuts cruel and heartless. Operators of nursing homes threatened to evict Medi-Cal patients. Other providers of service said they would drop out of the program. County boards of supervisors declared the state was shifting the cost of welfare medical services to those who pay county property taxes, since care of the indigent sick is a county responsibility under the California Constitution. The California Medical Association and county boards of supervisors instituted lawsuits against the state to cause the cuts to be rescinded.

---

*At a press conference announcing the cutbacks, Dr. Earl W. Brian, director of the Department of Health Care Services, said that many of the sought-after "postponed" services will never be provided since the Reagan Administration hopes for a complete revamping of the Medi-Cal system into something akin to a private insurance medical plan, according to the San Francisco *Chronicle* (December 3, 1970) p. 1.

**The Department of Health Care Services immediately began to recruit additional physicians as Medi-Cal consultants, at beginning salaries ranging from $20,496 to $27,456 per year.

COMMUNITY HEALTH CENTERS

One of the more recent approaches to delivery of health care to the poor has been the neighborhood health center concept.[14] Neighborhood health centers are local clinics offering a wide range of family-oriented outpatient medical services and preventive care for populations of about 15,000 to 30,000. The intent is to offer comprehensive care in the neighborhood and to give the residents a voice in the center's affairs.*

Through the neighborhood health center, the family can get treatment from practitioners of general medicine and the major specialties, preventive health services (such as physical checkups, presymptom screening, immunization, health education and family planning), diagnostic services, at-home care for chronic illness, rehabilitation services, dental care, mental health services, drugs and appliances, and transportation service in some cases. Under the program plan, needed hospitalization would be arranged at the center, and the patient's personal physician would continue medical responsibility for him.[15]

Program goals call for organization of professional personnel at each center into a number of "teams" composed of an internist, pediatrician, public health nurse, social worker and family health worker, with members of a family served by the same team of practitioners.

---

*Neighborhood health centers were first sponsored by the community action program of the Office of Economic Opportunity (OEO), under the 1966 amendments to the Economic Opportunity Act (PL 89-794) and by the U.S. Public Health Service under the Partnership for Health Program of 1967 (PL 90-174, sec. 314e). In August 1970 there were 83 neighborhood health centers throughout the country sponsored by the Office of Health Affairs of the Office of Economic Opportunity and 54 centers sponsored by the Public Health Service.

The original "war on poverty" did not include health among its priorities but it was soon realized that physical disabilities and illness of the participants were barriers to jobfinding and to learning. It was not until the Economic Opportunity Act of 1964 was amended in 1966 that health became an important priority.[16]

OEO and Public Health Service Centers

OEO guidelines call for a one-door center providing comprehensive outpatient services from qualified professionals; training community residents in new jobs as health aides; and using community involvement in planning and conducting the program. Only persons living in the area may receive regular care at the center. Eligibility for free services may be based on the state Medicaid (Title XIX) standard or the OEO poverty-level standard (by size of family and location in either farm or nonfarm area). Where need for care is acute, determination of eligibility may be delayed.

Utilization and coordination of existing federal, state and other medical care programs are necessary. Most centers are now run by a community corporation, one-third of whose members are area residents and the rest medical personnel and civic leaders. The corporation decides on choice of location, selection of staff, determination of clinic hours and scope of services and eligibility for service to be provided. The older centers have been under the leadership of neighborhood advisory councils, half of whose members were area residents. The councils have functions similar to those of the community corporations.

Three OEO neighborhood health centers are located in the Bay Area: at Alviso in Santa Clara County, East Palo Alto in San Mateo County and in the Mission District of San Francisco.

The Alviso Community Clinic in Santa Clara County has provided services for a preponderantly low-income Mexican-American community since June 1967. Prior to the opening of the center, the closest outpatient facility was in Milpitas, eight miles away. The center structure is a former four-unit motel donated by the owner and moved to land donated by the city. A Ford Foundation grant helped pay for materials to renovate the structure, and community residents volunteered labor to renovate, remodel and landscape.

Services offered by the Alviso Community Clinic include all outpatient services within the scope of the staff of two physicians, plus dental services, preliminary laboratory work, minor x-ray, and drug dispensing. Ambulance and shuttle services (by drivers trained in first aid) transport patients from their homes to the nearest medical facility and back. Santa Clara Valley Community Medical Center, El Camino Hospital and Stanford Hospital provide specialists' and inpatient services.

The project is sponsored by the Alviso Community Service Organization Health Foundation.

The East Palo Alto Neighborhood Health Center provides services for approximately 12,000 residents in the East Palo Alto-East Menlo Park area of San Mateo County. The initial grant was given to the county's Human Resources Commission, which contracted medical and health services through the San Mateo Department of Public Health and Welfare. A new building, with a design that incorporates community ideas and desires, is being funded by the Group Practice Facilities Title XII of the National Housing Act of 1965.[17]

The policymaking body of the center is the community board of directors, two-thirds of whom are selected by the community and one-third are appointed professionals. The board is incorporated as a nonprofit community corporation.

The service pattern of the clinic is oriented to family diagnosis and management. Instead of the usual departmentalization, the clinic offers care in a case conference setting by three teams of physicians. A family chooses one of the teams and stays with it to assure continuity of care. Besides meeting the health needs of its service area residents--175 patient visits a day--the health center aims to provide training and upward professional mobility to clinic workers from the community.

The Mission Neighborhood Health Center, located in the Mission district of San Francisco, was organized by the Citizens' Health Affairs Program (CHAP), composed of physicians, dentists and residents of the district. The CHAP membership includes representatives of the San Francisco Medical and Dental Societies, the San Francisco Department of Public Health and other health professionals. The center also has the support of the University of California Medical School. A Neighborhood Health Council and a Medical Advisory Board, all residents or practitioners in the Mission, are represented on CHAP.[18]

The clinic opened for business in a cluster of trailers in a parking lot May 1, 1968, and then moved into a rented building pending construction of a permanent facility. A new building, financed by a seven-year FHA loan to be repaid from the center's budget, opened in April 1970.[19] The clinic area encompasses many Spanish-speaking residents as well as a large group of American Indians.

A bilingual staff of 125 includes physicians, dentists and an optometrist in addition to nurses, laboratory and x-ray technicians, social workers and health aides. All specialties are represented, including a full range of psychiatric services. Services are offered by "teams" of practitioners, each of which includes the primary physician, a dentist, public health nurse, vocational nurse, receptionist, social worker and neighborhood health aides.

The Mission Medical Coalition, a group of 140 private physicians in the district and St. Luke's Hospital, in March 1970 signed an agreement with the center to serve as a backup group to the center staff and to work in the clinic if needed. The group will also serve as consultant to the center's staff physicians, accept referrals, and institute an advanced teaching program for the clinic physicians. Patient visits per month averaged 3000 in 1970.

Two additional neighborhood health centers funded by the U.S. Public Health Service are located in the San Francisco Bay Area; one is at Hunter's Point in San Francisco and the other at West Oakland in Alameda County.

Hunter's Point-Bayview Community Health Service is a five-year pilot project that opened in November 1968. Unlike the OEO projects described above, it does not offer direct medical services. Its staff of public health nurses, social workers and psychologists, "social health technicians," aims to reach families receiving almost no medical care.

Sponsors of the project, the John Hale Medical Society and the San Francisco branch of the National Medical Association (a Black professional organization), pointed out at the beginning that many people in the area were probably eligible for Medi-Cal, Medicare or other public programs but had never learned how to obtain services. The community service offers to help pay medical bills of persons ineligible for public programs and without insurance.

Eight health teams worked out of the center in 1970. Each was composed of a public health nurse, a licensed vocational nurse, a social worker, three neighborhood health aides and a secretary. In a shift of direction, the center announced in February 1970 that it desired to set up a prepaid health care plan for subscribers in the community.[20] Plans are being developed for a clinic.

The West Oakland Community Health Center, opened in September 1969, is a comprehensive health care facility sponsored by the U.S. Public Health Service and owned wholly by a community corporation, the West Oakland Health Council, Inc.

A grant from the Public Health Service of $5 million over a five-year period provides salaries for health aides, a nutritionist, health educator and biostatistician, as well as funds to cover payment for medical services to medically needy persons who have no other coverage.

The land, the building and the equipment at the center were made available by a grant of $1.5 million from the Economic Development Administration (Department of Commerce). Half the grant is an outright gift and the remainder is a loan to be repaid with interest over a 40-year period.

Training of neighborhood health aides is funded by the Office of Economic Opportunity.

The West Oakland Health Council, Inc., the nonprofit organization that owns the facility, consists of approximately 75 residents of the area. The council elects a 12-member executive board that is responsible for policy and decisionmaking for the center.

Health services include medical, dental and eye care, also laboratory, x-ray, pharmacy, podiatry, physical therapy, family planning, mental health and ancillary services. The West Oakland Health Group, composed of practitioners at the center, works on a fee-for-service basis, at usual and customary rates, under a yearly contract with the West Oakland Health Council, Inc. In addition, each practitioner makes an individual contract with the council committing a specific number of hours to the center and agreeing to an administrative overhead fee that is deducted from the total revenue generated by the practitioner.

Center services are available to all comers. Patients are billed directly for services used, as in any private medical office. However, Medi-Cal, Medicare, and private health insurance cards are fully honored and welcomed. Financial aid is available for persons living in the target area who cannot afford to pay for their outpatient care. The center emphasizes that no one living in the area is denied service because of inability to pay.

COUNTY CARE OF MEDICALLY NEEDY PERSONS

As noted earlier, medically needy persons are those who have sufficient income for their day-to-day needs but not enough income or liquid resources to pay medical bills. If they are aged, blind, disabled or members of a family with dependent children, they may be eligible for some benefits under the Medi-Cal program described in the preceding section. If they fit into none of these categories and are not entitled to care under any other public program, they may be entitled to free, part-pay or installment payment care under a county-supported program.

For more than a century California law made county supervisors responsible for providing medical and hospital care to the "indigent sick and dependent poor." The county hospital was the chief purveyor of such care. In counties that had no hospital, or in which the hospital was limited to general medical or post-surgery care, or where the hospital maintained no outpatient clinics, medical care was furnished by a county physician responsible directly to the board of supervisors, or was purchased by the county welfare department. The state made no contribution to the cost of these services.

Eligibility for County Care

Each county set its own standards of eligibility for county care. Many would not admit a person with income, personal or real property valued above a specified sum. Others weighed all income and resources against need for family maintenance and diagnosis, prognosis and cost of care.* Where it was determined that an applicant could assume the burden of all or part of the cost, he was asked to sign an agreement to repay the county weekly or monthly until the debt was paid. If the applicant had insufficient resources even for time payments, he had to sign an agreement to pay the bill if ever he came into assets that would enable his doing so.** In virtually all counties the debt was secured by a county lien against the unencumbered portion of any real property possessed, including a residence. Liens were usually not enforced during the life of the recipient unless the property moved on the market, nor were the liens foreclosed after his death until there was no longer a surviving spouse or dependent child.

The fact that a big hospital bill could be paid off on an installment basis made it possible for many low-income families to get care at the county hospital that they could not have obtained at a private or voluntary hospital. This financial problem could also arise for a higher income family whose insurance benefits had been exhausted.***

---

*The question was whether a family should be forced to liquidate all its financial reserves to pay for illness, when timely care might prevent its members from subsequently becoming public charges.

**The applicant signed a waiver of the statute of limitations in most counties, so that "ever" sometimes meant an obligation "forever."

***The fact that this situation can occur often has led some insurance carriers to experiment with a plan under which the carrier pays all medical bills, including those noninsured, and the subscriber contracts to repay the plan for noninsured expenses, along with interest charges thereon, over a period of time. Robert D. Ellers, "Postpayment Medical Expense Coverage," *Blue Cross Reports*, Research Series 1 (September 1969).

In all but three of the nine counties, the practice in the Bay Area has been to admit all patients who could not get care elsewhere, if they were legal residents.* No fixed figure was set on the amount of income or resources beyond which an applicant would be refused care. Any income and resources were weighed against the cost of care and the maintenance need of the family, and the patient was billed in accordance with his ability to pay. This procedure was followed in Alameda, Contra Costa, San Francisco, Santa Clara, Solano and Sonoma counties. Three counties--Marin, Napa and San Mateo--placed a limitation on the amount of personal property an applicant could possess and on the value of his real property. No ceiling was placed on income.

In computing the amount that the patient could pay on his bill over a period of time, all counties used a minimum budget to measure family needs according to family size. All required a signed agreement to repay and all but San Mateo required a waiver of the statute of limitations. All required a lien on real property.

The 1957 statewide program for medical care of federal-state welfare recipients (PAMC) limited program benefits to out-of-hospital services, and the counties remained responsible for hospitalization of these recipients as well as for all medical care of medically needy persons. The 1960 Medical Assistance for the Aged (MAA) program relieved the counties of responsibility for hospital care for needy aged and blind persons.

Recipients of general relief and medically needy persons ineligible for PAMC or MAA benefits still remained the responsibility of county government. Enactment of the Medi-Cal program in 1965 did little to change this situation, with one exception. Under a complicated

---

*Nonresidents were also admitted as emergency cases, and if they were indigent, the county of origin was billed for their care. Legal residence was defined as three years in the state, of which one year immediately preceding was in the county.

formula known as the county option, the legislation made a guarantee to the counties in exchange for a larger contribution to Medi-Cal funds: The county taxpayer would not have to be responsible for any increase over 1964-65 levels in the cost of county medical services to needy persons (with adjustments for population increase). County costs did increase over the base year, in part because of wage demands, in part because of improved services, and chiefly because of general inflation. The result was that in addition to receiving payments for services rendered to Medi-Cal and Medicare patients, most county governments also received state payments covering the rise in costs under the provision described above.

County hospital into community hospital. The enabling Medi-Cal legislation, moreover, included another provision affecting county medical services. This authorized the county board of supervisors to transform the county hospital into a community service for those who could afford to pay as well as for medically needy persons. Previously, county hospitals were not legally open to full-pay patients except in certain situations. A number of county hospitals in the state are now operating as community hospitals. In the Bay Area, hospitals in five counties are now open to all patients.

Bay Area County Programs

County hospitals and clinics furnish care for medically needy persons who are ineligible for Medi-Cal. These are persons aged 18 through 64 who are not disabled or blind or members of intact families with an employed parent, no matter how low the income. Couples with no children in the home and too young for Old Age, Survivors and Disability Insurance (OASDI) benefits, and a growing number of middle-aged women and other unemployed single persons all become county responsibilities.

In 1970 five Bay Area counties admitted patients regardless of income level and resources and arranged for settlement of medical bills on the basis of the county's assessment of the patient's ability to pay.

Seven of the nine counties still required a lien on property to secure the debt,* and eight required a waiver of the statute of limitations. None had a durational residence requirement.

In computing the patient's liability for his medical bills, *Alameda County* used the maintenance budget established for families receiving aid to dependent children (AFDC), adjusted for such items as actual housing costs and work expenses. The Medi-Cal regulations regarding utilization of resources were used.** Income and resources above that required to meet family or individual need were considered available for paying the medical debt. In order to secure the debt, Alameda County not only took a lien on all real property, including the home then owned or thereafter acquired, but also required the patient to waive forever the statute of limitations.

About half the inpatients in Highland Hospital in 1970 were "county cases," that is, persons ineligible for either Medi-Cal or Medicare. More than 90 percent of the clinic patients fall into this category. In January 1970 the Alameda County Board of Supervisors voted to open the hospital to all patients and their physicians as a community hospital.

Contra Costa County medical institutions in 1970 were open to all who requested treatment, but patients had to use county medical staff.*** Between 25 and 30

---

*State law prohibits a lien on the property of persons eligible for Medi-Cal, a federal requirement under Title XIX of the Social Security Act (Medicaid) for states receiving the federal subsidy.

**Besides income, resources include savings accounts, surrender value of life insurance, stocks, bonds and real estate. The value of a home is exempted.

***The county hospital is the only one in the county that provides (a) physical rehabilitation services, (b) treatment of communicable diseases, mental illness, alcoholism and tuberculosis and (c) care for premature infants.

percent of the general medical patients in Contra Costa hospital and medical clinics in 1970 were ineligible for the Medi-Cal and Medicare programs.

The medical social services unit had among its responsibilities the determination of eligibility for free care and for setting the amount of payment for those patients with ability to pay. To determine ability to pay, the medical social worker measured income and resources against allowance for maintenance need of the individual or family. The maintenance budget was more liberal than the AFDC budget. A family of four, for example, was allowed $372 to $491 a month, as compared with an AFDC range of $247 to $311 for the same size family. (The Medi-Cal allowance then was $300 a month.) Real property owned, other than the home in which the family resided, had to be utilized and the income derived from it considered in estimating the periodic payment for medical care. Savings and invested capital, above the amount necessary to maintain the family for one month, were considered income.

Contra Costa County abolished the lien requirement. Moreover, clients were required to waive the statute of limitations for 10 years only.

Marin County purchased hospital care for medically indigent persons from local hospitals. For outpatient care, clinics were held daily at the Civic Center. To be eligible for county care, a person could possess no more than $600 in personal property and have no other real property than a home whose assessed valuation was no more than $5000. No ceiling was placed on income but in assessing ability to pay, the AFDC maintenance standard plus 10 percent was used. The county took a lien on the home and the patient agreed to waive the statute of limitations.

In 1970 the county was responsible for about 500 medically needy persons who were ineligible for the state program.

Napa County contracted with local hospitals for care of medically needy county patients and permitted its patients to use private doctors for out-of-hospital care. To be eligible for county medical care, an individual could not possess more than $50 in cash or own real property whose assessed valuation was more than $3000. The patient was required to waive the statute of limitations and to grant a lien on his home to secure the debt. In assessing ability to pay, the county used the AFDC maintenance budget.

About 150 to 200 medically needy persons who were ineligible for Medi-Cal or Medicare were under county care in early 1970.

Services at *San Francisco* General Hospital were limited to persons who could not get care elsewhere (except in emergencies). About 35 to 40 percent of the patients in 1970 were medically needy persons ineligible for other public programs.

San Francisco allowed a family of four $561 as maintenance before any liability was imposed. The maintenance standard ranged from $275 for a single person to $1004 for a family of nine, with $43 a month extra allowance if the family owned a home.

Personal property allowed as a reserve amounted to $1500 for a single person and $3000 for a family. Real property was allowed up to an assessed valuation of $5000, from which the home was exempted.

By 1970, San Francisco no longer took a lien on real property to secure a medical debt, but the bill was secured by a promissory note that waived the statute of limitations.

San Mateo County General Hospital admitted all patients regardless of income and resources but required that all personal and real property except the home, as well as all income in excess of county standards, be obligated for medical care.

Personal property could be reserved to $350 and real property to an assessed valuation of $2500. Household furniture and personal effects to the value of $500 and the surrender value of life insurance policies to $300 were exempted. Maintenance need was measured by a modified AFDC budget which permitted rent actually paid and accrued debts to be taken into account.

On admission to the hospital, patients were required to execute a "demand note," secured by a deed of trust on real property, for the specific amount of the bill. The admission agreement did not require a waiver of the statute of limitations.

About 60 percent of hospital patients and 50 percent of clinic patients (excluding psychiatric) in 1970 were ineligible for state or federal medical care programs.

The *Santa Clara* Valley Community Medical Center, formerly the county hospital, was open to all patients and their physicians. Where a patient could not pay his bill in full, credit was extended for periodic payments and the liability was based on a flexible maintenance standard and all income and resources. To secure the debt, the county took a lien on all present and future real estate holdings, and the patient waived the statute of limitations.

About half the persons using the medical center services in early 1970 were ineligible for Medi-Cal or Medicare.

For admission to the *Solano County* Hospital, a medically needy person could not own personal property valued at more than $350 or real property with an assessed valuation of more than $500. The AFDC maintenance budget was used as a guideline in assessing a person's ability to pay the county medical bill. Liens were taken on property for bills of $200 or more and the patient was required to waive the statute of limitations. About 60 percent of the patients were ineligible for Medi-Cal in 1970.

The *Sonoma County* Hospital had become a community hospital to which all patients were admitted. There were no ceilings on income or resources of applicants but a modified AFDC maintenance standard was used in deciding liability for medical bills. A lien on property was taken for the amount of the bill and the patient agreed to waive the statute of limitations. Thirty to 40 percent of those using services in 1970 were "county" patients, ineligible for Medi-Cal.

CHAPTER V

Public Policy Issues

The preceding chapters have demonstrated the great diversity of health care plans in the Bay Area, the fragmentation in delivery of medical services and the wide variety of arrangements for paying medical bills. The Bay Area is a microcosm of the nation in regard to delivery of and payment for medical care, and no problems are peculiar to this region. Thus any statement about the Bay Area's health care system (or lack of system) could apply to any other area of the state as well as to any state of the union.

Nationwide as well as locally, insurance protection is greatest for hospital care, surgery and in-hospital physician visits. A much lower proportion of the population has protection against cost of medical services outside the hospital. Coverage of charges by extended care facilities or nursing homes, or by visiting-nurse or home health services (services that can reduce the need for hospital care) is low.

Where reimbursement for physician visits is provided in a basic health care plan, the scheduled fee is frequently far less than the actual charge. Major medical policies, which provide most of the reimbursement for doctors' office and home visits, usually exclude coverage of physicians' services for routine physical examinations and annual health checkups. Most so-called health insurance is thus directed toward episodes of illness and not toward maintenance of health.

Present insurance, moreover, meets only a small proportion of individual expenditures for personal health care services. Although 80 percent of the U.S. civilian population may have health insurance of one type or another, 60 percent of private personal health care expenditures are out-of-pocket costs for noninsured services and the uncompensated portion of insured services.

Furthermore, the proportion of persons covered by insurance varies directly with income levels.[1] Among those with little or no coverage are the unemployed, such as seasonal workers and their dependents, all of whom lose insurance protection shortly after their employment ceases. Others uninsured include the catastrophically ill persons who have exhausted their insurance benefits, and unemployed persons with poverty-level incomes.

Catastrophic illness at almost any income level can reduce the patient and his family to welfare status. Take, for example, a case personally known to the author, of a young executive who has to have dialysis treatment twice a week. The bill for one month's service amounts to $2875. His major medical insurance covers 80 percent of the charge (after the deductible). Major medical policies carry a maximum payment clause--in this case $20,000. Assuming that the policy has not paid any other charges, the patient will be covered for less than nine months' treatment. In that period he will have paid out-of-pocket more than $5000 for dialysis alone and reduced his resources for support of his family. Unless he dies soon, or a miracle occurs, there is little doubt that before long the family will be applying for help under Medi-Cal and possibly welfare as well.

HEALTH CARE CRISIS

For many years, the chief problem appeared to be the financing of health care services, especially for the old and for the medically indigent. Enactment of Medicare and, to a limited extent, Medicaid, together with the rapid growth of voluntary insurance, seemed to many an ideal solution. Despite a national expenditure of $64 billion for health care, however, millions of Americans in 1969 were still without adequate care. This lack is reflected in statistics showing that in 20 foreign countries men have a higher life expectancy than in the United States, and that in 11 countries the same is true of women; that in terms of infant mortality the United States ranks 16th, and that the infant mortality rate among nonwhites is 58 percent higher than among whites. John W. Gardner, former Secretary of HEW and now chairman of the Urban Coalition, declares that much of the money spent by the nation on health care is wasted.[2]

Dr. Roger Egeberg, HEW Assistant Secretary for Health, says that our health care delivery system is overwhelmed by rising demand and inefficient use of health resources. "Everyone associated with the health care system, in government and out, must be ready to correct past failures, to give up outmoded practices, to begin the process of renewal and change."[3]

The conviction that good medical care is a right and not a privilege has become almost universal, and pressure for change in the delivery of health care has built up to a critical point.

In July 1969 President Nixon forecast a "massive crisis" within the next two or three years unless steps were taken promptly. At the same time, Robert H. Finch, then Secretary of HEW, declared that the nation's health resources were overtaxed and being used wastefully, and that inflation in health costs was grave.[4] A report issued by the secretary stated:

> Expansion of private and public financing for health services has created a demand for services far in excess of the capacity of our health system to respond.

> The result is a crippling inflation in medical costs causing vast increases in government health expenditures for little return, raising private health insurance premiums and reducing the purchasing power of the health dollar of our citizens....
>
> Our task now as a nation is to acknowledge the extreme urgency of the situation, to take certain steps to arrest the inflation that is paralyzing us, and to put into motion initiatives that ultimately will reshape the system.

The report went on to say that the problem was beyond remedy by the government alone and that much of the burden must be borne by the private sector.*

Senator Abraham Ribicoff, another former Secretary of HEW, has pointed out that the government in fiscal 1969 spent $18.3 billion on its health programs, but it had no overall policy guidelines to make sure that the funds were being used properly or were having the desired effect. Twenty-three federal agencies that have health funds, Ribicoff said, often use the money at cross purposes or duplicate one another's efforts. Some of the agencies do not even know the number of health programs they have in operation. The senator stressed the need for coordinating the health functions of the government and for setting national goals.[5]

---

*John G. Veneman, former California assemblyman and then undersecretary in HEW, was asked by a reporter how he equated the administration's statements on the health care crisis with its performance. "Well, I don't see the point of issuing a lot of rhetoric," Veneman replied. "The statements were made merely to call attention to the problems; they were not meant to solve them." (New York *Times*, January 12, 1970, p. 19.)

THE MEDICAL INDUSTRY

Fragmentation and lack of policy in Washington provide only part of the picture. The fact is that despite dramatic technical gains, medicine is a sick industry. Its organizational structure is obsolete and its practitioners show little willingness to aid in rational reorganization of the health care delivery system.[6]

Shortages and maldistribution of health manpower and facilities continue, and charges keep soaring. The price rise is double that of the general advance in the consumer price level. The resulting rise in health insurance premiums has led to vociferous expressions of consumer dissatisfaction, particularly among the large purchasers of care. In reply, spokesmen for the medical industry assert that high prices are caused by the pressure of rising demand for medical services (because of Medicare), relatively slow growth in the supply of physicians, higher wages paid by hospitals to traditionally low-paid employees, and the greater complexity of the medical care furnished.[7]

Opinion is spreading, however, that high costs could be reduced considerably were the industry run more efficiently. Nationwide, hospitals are still being built where there is no shortage of beds. Expensive equipment often lies idle because the service for which it is designed is also offered in nearby competing hospitals. Patients are kept in the hospital when they would be cared for as well or better in nursing homes or in their own homes. Patients are hospitalized for diagnostic tests that could be performed outside, and more often than not, patients are admitted to the hospital a day or even longer before they undergo surgery. And doctors are still performing tasks that could be done by persons with less training.[8]

"The current health system has serious organizational, financing, productivity and access problems," declared the task force studying the problems of Medicaid, "and significant changes in our delivery system are required."

> For two decades programs financing medical care, whether public or private, have been reinforcing traditional ways of providing service. The Task Force is convinced that it no longer makes sense to keep pouring new wine in old casks--some of which are leaking.[9]

More efficient deployment of medical manpower, improved distribution of health resources through areawide planning, encouragement of group practice of medicine, and more emphasis on preventive care are all reiterated as means of reducing the cost of medical care.

Dr. Leona Baumgartner, visiting professor at Harvard Medical School and former New York City Health Commissioner, calls for a well-financed program to remodel the health system.

> Aggressive planning for better use of scarce resources, merging of small inefficient hospitals, firm links of smaller community hospitals to larger regional medical centers, wider use of telecommunications to bring expertise to larger numbers, more ambulatory care, more group practice, more emphasis on early and preventive care, more "allied" health workers....[10]

Manpower

Even with federal programs that provide funds for medical and nursing education already under way, the shortage of personnel cannot soon be overcome.* The

---

*The Health Training Improvement Act, signed by President Nixon in November 1970, authorizes federal financing of training programs in allied health professions.

many years now required for training professional medical personnel and the public apathy for meeting the financial needs of medical education are barriers to immediate solution of the problem.*

The Carnegie Commission on Higher Education has proposed shortening the overall period of medical training from eight to six years for physicians and four to three years for dentists. It also called for development throughout the country of 126 health education centers that would relate medical training more effectively to the delivery of health care. Among other recommendations made by the commission were:

More opportunity for women and members of minority groups to become physicians, dentists and paramedical workers;

The development of nine new medical schools;

The establishment of a National Health Manpower Commission to review the total spectrum of health care personnel;

The creation of a voluntary national health services corps to bring improved health care service to low-income and rural areas;

More equitable distribution of the financial burden for medical care between federal and state governments among the states;

State grants to private medical schools to support the recommended changes; and

---

*Proposition 1, the $275 million California health sciences bond issue on the November 3, 1970 ballot, failed by a 3-2 margin. It would have expanded medical schools and health profession training at six University of California campuses.

The adoption of uniform medical and dental school tuition fees in the range of $1000 a year. (The commission recognized that tuitions represent only a fraction of the institutional educational costs, which can run as high as $16,000 a year per student. To meet this difference, the commission recommended grants of up to $4000 per student to institutions along with grants of equal amounts to needy students.)[11]

Wider use by the medical industry of professional and subprofessional health workers is being widely advocated. Training of such workers is shorter and less expensive than that of a physician. Under a physician's supervision, such workers can supplement and possibly take over functions previously performed only by the physician. Expansion of paramedical manpower would mean a greater division of labor, specialization of function and efficiency and economy in utilizing costly skills and equipment.

One largely untapped source of physicians' assistants is the group of medical corpsmen released from the armed forces.[12] Programs are being started to document the army corpsmen's experiences, thus cooperating with civilian institutions in the same area to match civilian needs to the supply of trained personnel as they leave the army. A program undertaken by the Santa Clara Medical Society, funded by a grant from the Office of Special Manpower Programs (U.S. Department of Labor), has the initial goal of helping at least 50 discharged medical corpsmen in the county to find jobs or further their education in the health fields.

A more specialized program, started by San Francisco's Pacific Medical Center and City College of San Francisco, will train students as orthopedic assistants. Graduates of the two-year program will assist the orthopedic surgeon in patient care in the cast room, operating room, emergency room, office and in the application of traction. The Program is funded by a grant from the U.S. Public Health Service.[13]

The California Legislature in 1970 authorized the state Board of Medical Examiners to set up a physicians' assistant program, recommending qualifications, training requirements and licensing procedures.

Organization. The pet shibboleths of the medical profession--free choice and fee for service--have been attacked as myths that inhibit rational reorganization of the industry. For example, Dr. Kerr L. White, chairman of the Department of Medical Care and Hospitals at Johns Hopkins School of Public Health, told Senator Ribicoff's committee that "complete freedom with respect to the opportunity any patient has to consult any physician is illusory." He went on to say:

> What we do need is to organize effective health service systems so that there is relative freedom of choice of physicians and systems, freedom for innovation, experimentation, and change....[14]

Dr. White also finds solo practice inhibiting to efficient service:

> A strong case can be made for the fact that the solo practice of medicine by physicians unassisted by nurses, ancillary health workers, social services and reliable laboratory facilities is antiquated, if not obsolete; it is certainly wasteful and may be dangerous. Solo practice is obsolete because it implies that the physician will be continuously available to his patients; few physicians now attempt to maintain that fiction. The solo practitioner is apt to use his own training and skills inefficiently, has no way of extending his services, and receives few stimuli to maintain standards.

> Studies of the work of solo practitioners suggest that standards tend to vary widely but frequently are low.[15]

Dr. White proposed changing the delivery of health services by creating new kinds of incentives: financial incentives that would encourage efficient and effective organization. He believed that competition between systems would provide the financial incentives needed to encourage prudent use of resources and services and to reward commitment and responsibility. A system of federal formula and incentive grants at every stage of the health services system could encourage what is best in contemporary health services and discourage what is poor, he said.

The committee also heard Dr. Martin Cherkasky, director of the Montefiore Hospital, New York, testify that a high quality modern hospital surrounded by group practice, nursing home and home care must be the heart of any medical care system.

> The hospital should be used for definitive diagnosis and the inpatient bed...only for the period of biological crisis. Solo fee-for-service should, in the long run...be phased out and ultimately all doctors should be on handsome salaries in hospital-based group practice....A series of neighborhood hospitals should be related to a major teaching core hospital and the core hospitals to the medical school. Complex procedures, specialty education and research should be centered in the core hospital and medical school. Hospital care would be regionalized... with the consequent elimination of duplication of services and

> full uses of the opportunities to centralize.[16]

Although Dr. Cherkasky's view of a hospital-centered health care system is widely supported, it should be noted that a great many health professionals advocate family-centered health care through community-sponsored health care centers in which the hospital would form a part of the complex but not the dominating unit.[17]

Group Practice Advocates

Attention is often directed to the advantages inherent in group practice and particularly in that form of group practice that offers comprehensive prepaid care. Such plans are offered by groups of physicians who provide services in more than one medical field or specialty, with income from medical practice pooled and redistributed to the members according to some prearrangement. The group jointly uses technical personnel and equipment and centralized administrative and financial organization, greatly decreasing its costs of operation.

In 1967 the Department of Health, Education, and Welfare recommended that group practice, especially prepaid group practice, be encouraged.[18] "Groups of doctors practicing together can make more efficient use of equipment, auxiliary personnel and consultation than doctors practicing alone," the report stated. "Where the patient has paid in advance for comprehensive medical care under a group practice plan, less incentive exists to use high-cost hospital services where lower cost alternatives would meet the patient's needs just as well."

The utilization rate for nonmaternity hospitalization under the federal employees health benefits program (in the contract term ended December 31, 1965) was 415 days per 1000 members of the group practice plan, compared with 924 days for Blue Cross-Blue Shield subscribers, and 945 days for those covered by commercial insurance companies.[19]

Beneficiaries of the California State Employees' Hospital and Medical Care Act also use fewer hospital days in comprehensive group practice prepayment plans than in either the statewide service plans or the indemnity plans, according to a recent survey. The figures for days of hospitalization per 1000 beneficiaries per year, excluding maternity cases, are:[20]

Comprehensive group practice plans	770
Statewide service plans	945
Indemnity plans	1005
Individual practice plans	1281

The survey also showed that out-of-pocket charges for active employees' group practice plans were much lower than for any other type of plan.[21]

Some Objections

Several studies on patient attitudes and satisfaction indicate, however, that group practice prepayment plans often fall short of meeting the expectations of their memberships. The most common criticisms relate to failure of communication between member and plan, to impersonal attitudes on the part of professional and other personnel and to long waiting periods for appointments.[22]

Some experts question, moreover, whether widespread group practice will bring about more efficient organization of the medical industry since there has been little empirical evidence of economies of scale in physician practices. Richard M. Bailey, Associate Professor of Health Economics at the University of California, Berkeley, for example, believes that income gains in group practices arise from other medical services (such as x-ray and laboratory tests) offered by the group rather than from any increase in physician productivity.[23]

Nevertheless, from the point of view of savings in total cost to the community, group practice prepayment plans appear to score a success, particularly in reducing the cost of hospital care, as pointed out above. Harold F. Newman, director of the Group Health Cooperative of Puget Sound, compared hospital costs for Medicare patients throughout the country with those for Medicare members of his plan and found that cost per admission for his members was more than $200 lower. Although cost per enrollee-year for Medicare's supplementary medical insurance was $6 higher for Group Health members, Dr. Newman estimated that net savings to the Medicare program for his members amounted to $384,884.[24]

Planning

How can rational reorganization of health care be achieved? Assuming that a strong leadership in the medical industry is convinced it is necessary, then regional and areawide planning must be introduced to effect coherent interrelation of services and facilities. A joint committee of the American Hospital Association and the Public Health Service stated:

> Sound planning on an areawide basis can help to stem the rapid rise in costs of both capital construction and subsequent operation of our facilities. Moreover, it can help the development of a system of facilities and services to provide efficient and high quality of care. Under such a system, the individual facility would continue to be independently operated but would be

> encouraged to broaden its responsibilities by participating in areawide planning and by helping in carrying out such planning.[25]

Legislation

An attempt to foster such planning was generated by the Comprehensive Health Planning and Public Health Service Act of 1966 (PL 89-749). Federal grants were offered for two years to support comprehensive planning for health services, health manpower and health facilities on the state and local levels. Emphasis was given to the marshaling of all health resources--national, state and local, public and voluntary--in order to promote the highest level of health attainable for every person. The program envisaged a partnership for health that would draw into planning not only the health professionals but also the consuming public. Congress extended and expanded the grants for planning in 1967 under a bill known as the "Partnership for Health Amendments of 1967," signed by President Lyndon Johnson, December 5, 1967 (PL 90-174).

Further Needs

The legislation assumes that all portions of the economy that deliver health care will cooperate in providing care in the most economic manner possible to the entire community. However, abuses in the medical industry have been developing for years and it could take as many years to eliminate them completely. The HEW Secretary's Committee on Hospital Effectiveness in 1968 stressed that planning must be "applied in massive doses over the entire surface of the health service economy."

> Planning must be based on careful estimates and projection of needs for the whole spectrum of health

> services and must include appropriate representation of consumer as well as professional interests in the community.[26]

The committee suggested a link between planning and licensure. Effectiveness of licensure would be enhanced if minimum standards required for licensing were to include consideration of program and quality as well as facilities, the report said. New and added programs and facilities should represent useful increments to the health care system as seen by appropriate planning bodies. Specifically the committee advised that every health service institution be included in the jurisdiction of an areawide health service planning agency. It recommended that state licensing statutes for health facilities require prior review and approval of any change in physical facilities that significantly affect the nature or magnitude of the program of any health care institution.[27]

Many of the severest problems of the health service, the report declares, have their roots in financing methods and practices that have become embedded in hospital tradition and thought and have remained unchanged long after they have been widely recognized as barriers to hospital effectiveness.

> Thus lack of system and duplication of services and facilities owe their protracted existence in part to continued tax exemption and community support and unregulated freedom of institutions whose use of capital resources may be well intentioned but is often ill advised; high-cost services prevail where low-cost services would suffice because of prepayment and insurance practices that are contrary to the interests of the

> health economy; management inefficiencies are not only permitted but positively invited by cost reimbursement formulas that may reward spending and blink at extravagance.[28]

CONSUMER POWER

How much longer people will be able to meet the ever-mounting cost of health care through private insurance is difficult to tell. In any case, a long period of protracted unemployment that would deprive people of employment-related insurance coverage would alter any forecast. The issue, said Walter J. McNerney, president of the Blue Cross Association, at a HEW conference on private health insurance:

> boils down to what can be done to change the present system of financing health services so that its challenges of productivity, access and effectiveness are met, its strengths are preserved, and its anachronisms are discarded.[29]

Collective Purchasing

One way to improve the effectiveness of voluntary health insurance would be for major group purchasers to exercise their collective buying power, Joseph W. Ehrenreich, then Director of the research institute for business and economics at the University of Southern California, declared at the same conference.[30] Group purchasers can press for plans that are more comprehensive and can take more initiative in developing detailed specifications of what they want in a prepaid health plan, either indemnity or service type, Mr. Ehrenreich asserted. Some large groups have been conspicuously successful in doing this, usually because of union pressures exercised through the collective bargaining process. But in general the group purchaser still relies upon third parties for development of package plans and for proposals.

> Group purchasers, in so doing, invite confusion and nonrationality because they cannot usually make knowledgeable cost-benefit analyses of the different proposals. It would be much simpler to specify what is wanted and then obtain bids from several third parties. This would tend to force the third parties to compete on economic grounds, with all the concomitant pressures for cost control and more efficiency.[31]

Third parties, he said, are less than effective in controlling either vendor prices or quality of care, but large group purchasers can wield great influence with sellers. If other methods failed to control costs, then many giant unions and many giant business firms that have shown high interest in health care could combine to create a national chain of prepayment group practice centers, with hospital, convalescent home and nursing home affiliates. If these centers were open to the community, they would certainly provide a potent competitive force in the marketplace--one that existing providers could not ignore in setting their fees.[32]

Ehrenreich believes that the rising prices of health care stem to a large extent from the noncompetitive markets in which physicians and hospitals operate. He thinks that this is reflected in the physician's almost unilateral control of his fees and in the hospitals' ability to continue to operate with little record for economic rationality.

> Fundamentally, there is a need for reinstitutionalizing the health care

> industry to place the physicans and hospitals in a posture vis-à-vis the consumer that is more typical of sellers and buyers in other markets.[33]

Consumer Participation in Policymaking

Isolation from knowledge about the medical and health needs of a population is a possible consequence of denying the ultimate user of health care services a role in the policy-making process, according to the Task Force on Medicaid and Related Programs.* The task force recommended that any board or group set up to advise policy-making officials at any level of government should provide for consumer representation and that consumer members should reflect the social, economic, racial and geographic characteristics of their communities. This would also apply to committees and subcommittees of such boards as well as to any federally funded or operated health programs.

Proprietary organizations and institutions concerned with health care services should be encouraged to provide for consumer involvement in monitoring their services, the task force said.[34]

Labor Leadership

Broad coalitions of management and/or labor could no doubt negotiate directly with the vendors of health care, stimulate effectiveness in community health planning groups and institute cost controls. Labor unions

---

*The task force was established by former Secretary of HEW, Robert H. Finch. The chairman was Walter J. McNerney, President of the Blue Cross Association. The group included representatives of industry, labor, consumers, the health and social sciences and health institutional and service groups.

nationwide are being driven by high costs and a growing awareness of quality to look much more critically at their medical care programs. If the money now being paid out for these programs were harnessed to plans for meeting the hospital and medical care needs of the community, leaders say, the requisites would be available to bring about necessary changes in the medical care establishment. They appear ready to repudiate the voluntary insurance approach to health care. The late Walter Reuther, President of the United Auto Workers, voiced a widespread sentiment when he declared:

> The insurance industry has worked hard. They have made a constructive contribution over the years. It has become increasingly obvious, however, that the health care crisis in America is beyond the insurance industry's capability of controlling costs while medical costs are pyramiding. They lack the capability of assuring quality. They lack the capability of providing universal coverage.
>
> We live in the space age...yet we are traveling in a Model T economic vehicle with respect to the organization of health care. As an old automobile worker, I can tell you that the old model needs more than a tuneup or a new set of spark plugs. The old model should be respectfully relegated to its proper place in the archives of America's social history. It should be replaced with a new model that reflects the greater needs and the new economic realities of the world in which we live.[35]

California Council for Health Plan Alternatives

The council was established by California's major unions to seek out and bargain for more effective means of organizing, operating and financing health services. An underlying assumption is that, whereas more money will be needed to do the job, much more can be done with the money now being spent.

Although collectively bargained plans have been in the forefront of employee health care programs, negotiated plans that provide comprehensive care for both employee and dependents with minimum out-of-pocket costs are few. An analysis, *Health Plan Grading System* (1969), of nine large labor-management health care plans in California written under voluntary insurance found the plans to be seriously wanting, measured against a yardstick of quality care (Chart 2, p. 17). The study found that the highest priced health plans do not necessarily provide the best care. The "yardstick for evaluation" was designed by a team led by Dr. Lester Breslow at the School of Public Health, University of California, Los Angeles, under a grant from the California Council for Health Plan Alternatives. The yardstick sets up a grading system that assigns points to a health plan according to scope of benefits, coverage of dependents, quality protections, control of out-of-pocket expenses and strength of administrative arrangements. The council seeks to develop standardized plans at different premium levels so that unions can adopt the plans and ask for competitive bidding.

Further rises in health care premiums have led the council to press for tighter state regulation over hospitals. It rejects the contention that wage increases forced by unionized hospital workers justify recent increases in hospital daily rates. The council maintains that rate increases more likely "result directly from wasteful and inefficient hospital and physician practices" and that the public should be allowed to find out the facts. It asserts that hospitals should be compelled to justify their increases in public hearings.

"No other industry essential to our lives is allowed to operate without public accountability," the council says.[36]

The council supported legislation introduced by State Senator Anthony C. Beilenson in the 1970 California Legislature. The measure would place hospitals and other health care institutions under greater public regulation and scrutiny. Comprehensive health planning bodies would be authorized to hold hearings and pass on proposed rate increases, and require hospitals to disclose publicly all details of their costs and operations.[37]

Gordon R. Cumming, administrator of Sacramento County Hospital and past President of the California Hospital Association, has also proposed creation of a public utilities type of state commission to regulate hospital charges, services and new construction. "We must recognize that hospitals have a public nature, regardless of their ownership," he told the association's annual meeting. Mr. Cumming thinks that a voluntary system will not work. "I'm not against a voluntary system," he said, "but we need more sinew than sweet talk and persuasion."[38]

Reuther Committee for National Health Insurance

Delegates from labor unions, church groups and medical organizations met in October 1969 to discuss a proposal for universal health insurance administered by a new Office of National Health Insurance Administration in the Department of Health, Education, and Welfare.[39] The plan would replace Medicare and Medicaid and eliminate the need for private health insurance except where insurance might cover some medical expense not included in the federal program.

Costs of the plan would be financed by payroll taxes similar to existing Social Security taxes. The division of the tax between employers and employees would be a matter of collective bargaining. The remaining share of the cost would be borne by federal general tax revenues.

Doctors and hospitals would be paid directly by the national plan. Physicians in private practice could choose their method of payment: fee for service, salary, capitation or some other method. Incentives would be provided, however, to move away from solo practice fee-for-service payments "toward hospital-affiliated or hospital-based medical groups in order to stimulate better organization within and between institutions."*

HEALTH INSURANCE UNDER SOCIAL SECURITY

Under present haphazard arrangements for paying for medical services, costs of administration are increased by the duplication of selling, accounting, claims review and other organizational expenses. For instance, in 1966 there were more than 700 commercial insurance companies selling health insurance. The cost of administering the various nongovernmental plans ran as high as 50 percent of the total premiums for some companies.[40]

Wilbur Cohen, former HEW Secretary, has pointed out that in 1968 it took almost 15 percent of the $12.9 billion premium income of all carriers, commercial and voluntary, to administer the health insurance programs. A national plan using the existing Social Security collecting system instead of the hundreds of separate collecting units of private plans, Mr. Cohen said, could probably reduce total administrative costs by about one-third. He estimated that a comprehensive national insurance plan would probably involve $35 to $40 billion in medical expenditures, and use of the Social Security collection mechanism could save $1 to $2 billion a year in administrative expenses.[41]

---

*For further details on the plan, see table, "Comparison of Five Proposals for National Health Insurance," pp. 150-151.

The United States is the only industrialized country in the world that does not have national health insurance or a public medical service covering all or nearly all of the population. Although health insurance legislation was considered by 20 states in the period 1914-1920, the movement was quiescent until the late 1930s. Advocacy of national health insurance with universal coverage, at that time, led to Medicare 20 years later.

In January 1967, 51 percent of the American public were in favor of a federal medical plan for the entire population, similar to Medicare for the aged, according to a public opinion poll.[42] Opposed were 39 percent, and 10 percent had not decided. In view of the 26 percent increase in the cost of medical services in the following four years--almost double the rise in the general price level--and the continuing rise, it is not unlikely that a current opinion poll would substantially increase the majority in favor of universal health insurance, administered by Social Security.

With a handful of dissenting votes, the National Governors' Conference meeting at Colorado Springs in September 1969 endorsed a policy statement calling on the federal government to adopt a nationwide program of compulsory health insurance, coupled with hospital cost controls as the primary method of keeping rising health costs from preventing all people from receiving the medical care they need.* The statement was presented by the Committee on Human Resources of the National Governors' Conference, of which Governor Nelson Rockefeller of New York was chairman. Essentially the proposal called for financing health insurance purchased from

---

*A resolution adopted by the Association of American Physicians and Surgeons in October 1969 condemned the conference action, declaring that it was "maneuvered" through the conference by "questionable methods...contrary to the will of the majority." See "AAPS Convention Resolutions," *Medical Care Review*, 26(11): 1113-1117 (1969), esp. p. 1116.

private insurance companies, by employer-employee contributions through payroll deductions. Self-employed and unemployed persons above the poverty level would pay the full premium themselves. The elderly would be cared for through Medicare, and the federal government would purchase the insurance for people below the poverty level.[43]

NEW YORK STATE PROPOSALS

Governor Rockefeller has been advocating compulsory health insurance in his own state for over a decade. In 1959 he proposed to the state Legislature a program requiring every employer to buy major medical insurance for his employees. Insurance purchased from private carriers would have supplemented basic health plans and paid customary fees without a fee schedule. The state would have underwritten any group that for some reason could not get private coverage. State employees in New York had major medical policies; the state paid 50 percent of the premium for the individual employee and 35 percent of the additional family cost. The governor's proposal to make major medical insurance compulsory for all workers and employees in the state was not approved by the Legislature.

Again in 1967 Governor Rockefeller proposed a compulsory health insurance law (that also failed) which would require every employer with three or more workers to provide basic hospital and surgical coverage for workers and their families. Insurance would have been underwritten by private carriers. Cost of premiums was to be divided equally between the employer and employee but the employee's contribution could not exceed 2 percent of his salary. Employers would have been authorized to pay all or part of their employees' share.[44]

PAST PROPOSALS IN CALIFORNIA

Although New York has taken the lead, California was once in the forefront as an advocate of public health insurance. As far back as 1915, Republican Governor Hiram Johnson created a state commission for the study of social insurance. The commission produced and collected 300 pages of evidence, held public hearings and reported unanimously in favor of compulsory health insurance for "wageworkers and other persons of small income." The commission proposed submitting to the voters a constitutional amendment to empower the Legislature to establish a health insurance system, either voluntary or compulsory, for persons whose incomes it judged insufficient to meet the costs of illness.

In April 1917, the Legislature voted to place the amendment on the ballot. It passed the Assembly on the first vote; in the Senate it first was defeated, then reintroduced the next day and passed overwhelmingly. Of course, a vote to put the measure on the ballot was not necessarily a vote in favor of health insurance. Despite support by Hiram Johnson, by then a U.S. senator, and William Stephens, a Republican governor, voters defeated the amendment 3-1.

A compulsory health insurance bill was introduced again in 1935 but was defeated in the Senate. In 1939 Democratic Governor Culbert Olson backed an insurance bill that was defeated in the Assembly. A number of bills advocating a state plan for health insurance were introduced in the 1945 Legislature. One plan, sponsored by Republican Governor Earl Warren, would have been supported by a payroll tax and administered through unemployment insurance. Hearings were held and studies made by the Assembly public health committee, but the bill died in committee. Governor Warren continued to advocate a state program for prepaid medical care, but with no success.

FEDERAL MOVES

Robert H. Finch, then Secretary of HEW, in September 1969 directed the Task Force on Medicaid also to take a hard look at the costs and possible benefits of a Medicare program for all ages.[45] The administration's interest in national health insurance, which Mr. Nixon opposed during his successful presidential campaign, stems from attempts to cope with the ever-increasing costs of the Medicaid program. Studies of the cost to the federal government of a national health insurance system were being made in the Treasury Department and by HEW in 1969 and 1970.

First Attempts

Interest on the part of the federal government in national health insurance under Social Security is not new. A National Health Conference called in 1938 by the federal interdepartmental committee to coordinate health and welfare activities recommended among other things consideration of a comprehensive program designed to increase and improve medical services for the entire population. To finance such a program, the conference advised both funds drawn from general taxation and specific insurance contributions from potential beneficiaries.[46]

Companion bills, providing for a comprehensive postwar social security program, including a national health insurance plan financed through a payroll tax, were introduced in 1943 by Senator James Murray (Montana) and Senator Robert Wagner (New York) and also by Congressman John Dingell (Michigan). The proposal died in committee although it was strongly supported by organized labor.

In 1944 the "economic bill of rights" included in President Roosevelt's state of the union message, specified the right to "adequate medical care," and the eighth annual report of the Social Security Board called for compulsory health insurance.

In May 1945, Senators Murray and Wagner introduced S. 1050 which was similar to their 1943 bill. Later in the same year President Harry Truman proposed a broad legislative program for national health insurance, and the two senators introduced S. 1606, known as the National Health Act of 1945. Title I provided for expansion of public health services, maternal and child health services, and the medical care of needy persons. Title II provided for a system of personal health services to be developed on a social insurance basis. Congressman Dingell introduced a companion bill in the House.

The program would have covered physicians' services, hospital, nursing, laboratory and dental services, with free choice of physician and hospital. It was to be financed by a 4 percent increase in the Social Security contribution and by use of general revenue funds for those not covered. Federal grants would have enabled the states to provide care for persons unable to pay and to contribute part of private health insurance premiums for other needy persons.

Extensive hearings were held by the Senate Committee on Labor and Education in 1946, but no action was taken by Congress.

Truman's Efforts

President Truman's three major messages to the 80th Congress--the state of the union message, the budget message and the economic report--all called attention to the need for health insurance. The President submitted a broad public health program and recommended that the Congress lay the legislative groundwork for a national system of compulsory health insurance. Again in May 1947, in a special message on health, he called attention to the health needs of the nation and recommended enactment of a broad national health program. These recommendations were in line with popular opinion of the time. A number of polls had indicated growing interest in a comprehensive health program and particularly in a system for prepayment of medical costs.

Senators Murray, Wagner and Claude Pepper (Florida) introduced S. 1320, and a companion bill was introduced in the House by Representative Dingell. The bill took into consideration suggestions made during the hearings on S. 1606. Among other provisions, the new measure would have made available a comprehensive national system of prepaid personal health services, with decentralized administration to be carried out by the states and by local agencies, and authorization to use federal grants-in-aid to the states toward paying for personal health services furnished to needy persons. Hearings were conducted but no action was taken.

In 1949, President Truman called yet again for a national health insurance plan financed by Social Security taxes, and the Murray-Wagner-Dingell bills were once more introduced as S. 1679 and H.R. 4312. Hearings by congressional committees evoked sharp controversy. Organized labor, many northern Democratic congressmen and private organizations of professional workers in the social welfare field favored broad federal responsibility in this area. Strongly opposed were the American Medical Association, the American Dental Association, the American Pharmaceutical Association, Blue Cross-Blue Shield commissions, the U.S. Chamber of Commerce, the American Legion, the Farm Bureau Federation, National Grange, Health Insurance Council, Health and Accident Underwriters Conference, and others. No action was taken on either bill.[47]

RENEWED PRESSURES

Once again there is a deep and growing interest in national health insurance. Conceivably, the total cost of a comprehensive national program might not be more than total present expenditures for health services by individuals, both personally and through voluntary insurance, and by the myriad of governmental programs.

Testimony before Senator Ribicoff's committee on behalf of the AFL-CIO executive council in April 1969 asserted that national health insurance could provide a sound financial foundation for the rational organization of a medical care system. The council proposed:

> Early consideration by the Congress of a universal National Health Insurance program under Social Security to be financed on a tripartite basis, that is: one-third of the cost to be paid by the employee, one-third by the employer and one-third from the Federal general revenues. Methods of reimbursement to providers of care must be flexible and not only allow, but encourage, the use of capitation as the preferred method of physician and hospital payments.[48]

The council on that occasion saw national health insurance as taking a long time in the legislative process. It therefore presented a number of proposals calling for immediate action. Among these were: (1) immediate extension of Medicare to the disabled and as rapidly as possible to all Social Security beneficiaries; (2) improvement of Medicare. The latter proposal would (1) cover a wider gamut of health needs and services, including prescription drugs, eyeglasses and hearing aids, therapeutic appliances, dental care and preventive care; (2) eliminate financial deterrents to care, such as deductibles and coinsurance; (3) merge part A (hospital benefits) and part B (medical benefits) into a single health care program financed on a tripartite basis on Social Security principles; and (4) eliminate the requirement for fiscal intermediaries "which unnecessarily complicates and adds to the cost of the program."[49]

By September 1970, however, the AFL-CIO was convinced it should use all its political muscle to push national health insurance through the 1971 Congress. President George Meany told Senator Jacob K. Javits (Rep. New York):

> This isn't something a group of labor leaders decided on....The pressure is coming on us from the bottom of the economic and social structure.[50]

Provision of national health insurance in the United States appears to be an idea whose time has come. The need for such a plan is now seldom questioned. The problem is, what kind of plan? Here, wide differences of opinion exist. Five plans illustrating different approaches to a national program, all with significant sponsorship, were analyzed by the Social Security Administration in 1970.[51] These were: (1) Griffiths bill (H.R. 15779): (2) Committee for National Health Insurance (Health Security Program); (3) Javits bill (S. 3711); (4) American Medical Association "Medicredit" plan; (5) Pettengill-Aetna proposal.

The table on pp. 150-151 outlines the principal characteristics of the five proposals and is taken from the Social Security Administration analysis referred to above.*

The Griffiths and Committee for National Health Insurance proposals were in the social insurance tradition in that they proposed virtually universal coverage, federal government administration and financing in part by social insurance contributions. The AMA and Aetna Insurance Company proposals were for private insurance, with coverage on a voluntary basis, administered by the private carriers (supervised by government), and financed from private sources and governmental general revenues. The Javits bill, incorporating elements of both approaches, provided for a universal federal program based on

---

*R & S Note No. 12-1970 (pp. 150-151 and note 51 above) also contains a bibliography designed to furnish additional information on the five proposals, on other proposals and on the general subject of national health insurance.

COMPARISON OF FIVE PROPOSALS FOR NATIONAL HEALTH INSURANCE

SUBJECT	GRIFFITHS BILL	COMMITTEE FOR NATIONAL HEALTH INSURANCE
GENERAL APPROACH	Government universal health insurance program financed by payroll tax and general revenues.	Government universal health insurance program financed by payroll tax and general revenues.
COVERAGE	U.S. residents.	U.S. residents.
BENEFITS	Comprehensive health benefits. Major exclusion is dental services for adults. No cost-sharing except for physician, dentist, and other ambulatory services. ($2 copay per visit, with certain exceptions.)	Comprehensive health benefits. Major exclusion is dental services for adults. Limitations on drugs and nursing-home and mental health care. No cost-sharing.
ADMINISTRATION	Federal board composed of HEW officials and nongovernment members; regional offices; advisory bodies.	Federal board under Department of HEW; regional offices; advisory bodies.
PAYMENT OF PROVIDERS	*Physician and dentist groups* can contract to receive predetermined payment and pay their members as they choose (including fee for service). *Individual primary physicians and dentists* may elect per capita, salary, or combination of methods and receive an allowance to pay for services of specialists and other health professionals. *Hospitals:* Negotiated budget that includes allowance for nursing-home and home health services.	*Physicians and dentists:* Regional funds allocated first to those in group practice or selecting capitation, salary, or per session basis. Residual allocated to local payment authorities to pay those selecting fee-for-service or per case basis. *Hospitals, nursing homes, home health agencies:* Negotiated budget designed to pay reasonable cost under efficient organization.
FINANCING	Tax equal to 7 percent of payroll, including 1 percent on employees, 3 percent on employers, and a payment from general revenues equal to 3 percent. Earnings base of $15,000, adjusted automatically to increases in wage levels.	Tax equal to about 7-3/4 percent (on 1969 basis) including 2.8 percent on employers, 1.8 percent on employees and on nonwage income, and general revenues payment equal to 3.1 percent. Tax levied on first $15,000 of employees and nonwage income combined, and on total payroll for employers.
COST	Cost would have been $35.8 billion in fiscal 1969, according to AFL-CIO.	Cost would have been $37 billion in fiscal 1969, according to CNHI.

[1]Participants in approved employer-employee health plans and persons purchasing approved private insurance may remain outside of government plan and be exempted from payroll taxes.

[2]Amount of tax credit would be graduated from 100 percent to 10 percent, depending on the amount of tax liability on tax return. The maximum (100 percent) credit would be an amount equal to the premium cost of a qualified health insurance policy.

JAVITS BILL	AMA MEDICREDIT	PETTENGILL PROPOSAL
Government universal health insurance program (similar to Medicare) with option of "electing out" by purchase of private insurance.[1]	Income tax credits to offset cost of qualified private health insurance.[2]	Private insurance for poor or related groups through an insurance pool subsidized by government.[3]
U.S. residents.	U.S. residents.	Poor, near poor, and uninsurables (voluntary).
Same as Medicare (hospital, physician, nursing home, etc.--subject to cost-sharing and limitations). Also annual checkups, limited drugs, and dental care for children under age 8.	To be qualified, policy must include basic hospital and physician benefits, and may optionally offer supplementary drug, blood, hospital, and other benefits. Benefits subject generally to cost-sharing and limitations.	Statewide uniform benefits. Minimum benefits to be specified in Federal law and to include ambulatory and institutional care.
Department of HEW (as under Medicare) or, under contract with HEW, by State government. Processing of claims conducted by private carriers (as under Medicare) or, under certain conditions, by special quasi-government organizations.	Federal advisory board (including HEW, IRS, and non-government members) to establish Federal standards for use by State insurance departments in approving private insurance plans.	Statewide insurance pool administration by carrier selected by State with concurrence of Federal Government.
Until July 1, 1973, reasonable cost for hospital and institutions and reasonable charges for physicians (as under Medicare). Thereafter, new methods, developed in interim, may be employed.	Present methods under private insurance.	Present methods under private insurance.
Tax equal to 10 percent of payroll, including 3.3 percent on employers and 3.3 percent on employees, and payment from general revenues equal to 3.3 percent. Tax levied on $15,000 earnings base for employees and on total payroll for employers.	Financed from Federal general revenues.	Poor would pay no premium and the near poor and uninsurables would pay part of the premium. State and Federal general revenues would finance the balance of the cost of the program.
Cost of $66.4 billion in 1975, according to Social Security actuary.	Net cost for 1970 estimated at $8 billion by AMA and at $15 billion by SSA.	Estimates not available.

[3]Proposal also provides (a) a catastrophic protection plan, geared to family income, for the general population, and (b) encouragement for additional coverage under employment-related health insurance.

Source: U.S. Department of Health, Education, and Welfare, Social Security Administration, Office of Research and Statistics, *National Health Insurance: A Comparison of Five Proposals*, by Saul Waldman and Evelyn Peel, R & S Note No. 12 (Washington, D.C.: 1970), pp. 18-19.

social insurance but offered the alternative of opting out through purchase of approved private insurance coverage.

The Griffiths bill was essentially an AFL-CIO proposal sponsored by Congresswoman Martha Griffiths (Dem. Mich.) and cosponsored by 20 others from nine states. The bill would control costs by allowing providers to organize themselves into medical and dental groups, which would be responsible for fulfilling the contract with the government. The amount of the contract would set a budget within which doctors, dentists, hospitals and laboratories would have to operate. Excessive care and unnecessary services by providers would reduce their profits. Efficiency would show up as budget surpluses and greater profits. The medical and dental groups could pay their members in any way they chose, but the total of individual charges could not exceed the overall budget of the group.

The program of the Committee for National Health Insurance, outgrowth of Walter Reuther's Committee of 100 for National Health Insurance, was backed by Senators Kennedy, Cooper and Yarborough. Both plans strongly emphasized development of prepaid group practice programs, as did the Javits bill.

Provision for a "catastrophic coverage benefit" (similar to major medical plans) is made in the AMA and Pettengill plans.*

THE 1971 KENNEDY BILL--S. 3

Senate Bill No. 3, introduced in the 92d Congress by Senator Kennedy and others as the Health Security Act

---

*The Nixon administration in 1970 was considering a payroll tax to insure most Americans against catastrophic medical expenses. The Senate Finance Committee wrote such a provision into the pending Social Security Amendments.

of 1971, would provide payment for a broad range of health care services for all United States residents. Benefits cover prevention, treatment and rehabilitation, with some limitations. Coinsurance and deductibles are not required. Principal limitations are:

Dental care. Restricted to children through age 15 at beginning, with covered age group increasing to include persons through age 25.

Skilled nursing home care. Limited to 120 days, if home is not owned or managed by a hospital and payment for care is made through the hospital's budget.

Psychiatric care. Hospitalization limited to 45 consecutive days of active treatment during a benefit period; psychiatric consultations limited to 20 visits in benefit period.

Prescribed medicines. Not covered unless provided through a hospital or organized patient care program, or required for a chronic or long-term illness.

Financing

Half the cost of the program would come from federal general tax revenues; 36 percent from a tax of 3.5 percent on employer payrolls; 12 percent from a tax of one percent on employee wage and nonwage income up to $15,000 a year; and 2 percent of the cost would come from a 2.5 percent tax on self-employment income up to $15,000 a year. All moneys would be held by the Health Security Trust Fund.

Resources Development Fund. To improve the delivery of health care, a special fund would be established to support innovative health programs in such fields as manpower, education, training and group practice development. The Resources Development Fund would be supported by a $200 million congressional appropriation the first year and $400 million the second year prior to the start of benefit payments. Once the benefits begin, up to 5 percent of the trust fund would be set aside each year for resource development.

Incentives. Financial, professional and other incentives are built into the program to move the health care delivery system toward organized arrangements for patient care, and to encourage preventive care and early diagnosis of disease. Incentives are also used to provide quality health care in rural areas.

Administration

The program would be administered by a five-member Health Security Board in the Department of Health, Education, and Welfare. Provision is made for a National Health Security Advisory Council of 20 members. The majority must be representative of consumers and the others representative of providers of health services. All members are to be appointed by the secretary of HEW on recommendation of the Health Security Board. Consumer members are to be "persons not engaged in and having no financial interest in the furnishing of health services, who are familiar with the needs of various segments of the population for personal health services and are experienced in dealing with problems associated with the furnishing of such services." (S. 3, Sec. 125a) Similar provision is made for regional and local advisory councils, and professional and technical advisory committees drawn from the health professions.

Providers of medical services would be paid directly by the program, apparently eliminating the present Medicare system of using insurance carriers as intermediaries. Practitioners would be paid on the basis of fee for service, or if they so elect, by the capitation method, covering all medical services for a list of persons who have chosen that practitioner. Arrangements could also be made to pay an independent practitioner a full-time or part-time stipend in lieu of, or as a supplement to, the other methods of payment. Benefits would begin July 1, 1973.

PRESIDENT NIXON'S 1971 PROGRAM

President Nixon's message to Congress on national health care, delivered February 18, 1971, incorporated many proposals long offered by health care experts, although it differed substantially from the labor-backed Kennedy bill. Mr. Nixon rejected the concept of comprehensive health insurance through the Social Security mechanism and advocated instead a "national health partnership" with the private insurance companies.

> I believe that our government and our people, business and labor, the insurance industry and the health profession can work together in a national partnership to achieve our health objectives. I do not believe that the achievement of these objectives requires the nationalization of our health insurance industry.[52]

Plan for Employees

The heart of the Nixon program is a National Health Insurance Standards Act which would require employers to provide private health insurance coverage for their employees, beginning July 1, 1973. Exempted from the act are state and local governments, the self-employed and organizations or persons employing domestics or seasonal part-time workers. Premium costs would be shared by employer and employee, the employer paying 65 percent until 1976, when his share would rise to 75 percent.* Employees would pay the remaining share and also some amounts for deductibles and coinsurance.** The

---

*Insurance premiums for both employees and dependents were fully paid by half the Bay Area employers who replied to the questionnaire sent by the writer. See Ch. II, pp. 40-41.

**Deductibles would not apply to maternity or well-baby care.

deductible would be $100 per year per person with a maximum of three per family, plus the full cost of hospital daily charges for the first two days and 25 percent of the remainder after deductible.[53]

The minimum insurance package would include hospitalization, surgery, physician's visits both in the hospital and outside, full maternity and well-baby care (including immunizations), diagnostic x-ray and laboratory services, family planning, and a catastrophic illness clause that would pay up to $50,000 for each family member.[54]

Plan for Poor Persons

Mr. Nixon also proposed a new family health insurance plan for poor families not covered by the proposed insurance standards act and headed by unemployed, intermittently employed or self-employed persons, with a net income of less than $5000 for a family of four. Unemployed persons under the age of 65 and with no children would still not be covered. The federal government would pay all the insurance premiums for families with incomes under $3000 and some part for those with incomes from $3000 to $5000. The program would supplant Medicaid (Medi-Cal in California).

In addition, Mr. Nixon would require in each state establishment of special insurance pools that would offer insurance at reasonable group rates to people who did not qualify for other programs: the self-employed, for example, and poor-risk individuals who often cannot get insurance.[55]

Health Maintenance Organizations

As an alternative to paying separate fees for separate services, persons covered by the Nixon program would be given the choice of membership in a Health Maintenance Organization (HMO)--the current euphemism for prepaid comprehensive group practice. Public and private health insurance plans would be required to allow beneficiaries to join an HMO when one is available. Mr. Nixon pointed out:

> In recent years, a new method for delivering health services has achieved growing respect. This new approach has two essential attributes. It brings together a comprehensive range of medical services in a single organization so that the patient is assured of convenient access to all of them. And it provides needed services for a fixed contract fee which is paid in advance by all subscribers....
>
> Under traditional systems, doctors and hospitals are paid in effect on a piece work basis. The more illnesses they treat, and the more service they render, the more their income rises. This does not mean, of course, that they do any less than their very best to make people well. But it does mean that there is no economic incentive for them to concentrate on keeping people healthy.
>
> A fixed-price contract for comprehensive care reverses this illogical incentive. Under this arrangement, income grows not with the number of days a person is sick but with the number of days he is well.[56]

To stimulate growth of the Health Maintenance Organizations, the Nixon plan would provide $23 million for planning grants and federal guarantees of private loans for capital construction and for sustaining initial operating deficits until each HMO achieved optimum enrollment. Further federal grants and loans would subsidize establishment of HMOs in scarcity areas to help offset special risks and costs in such areas.[57]

Medicare. Medicare would continue for aged persons with some slight changes that would raise coinsurance payments and allow beneficiaries to join a health maintenance organization.

Personnel. The Nixon program also provides for expansion of loans to medical students and establishment of a national service agency to recruit medical personnel for slum and rural areas. Grants to medical and allied schools would be determined by the number of students the school graduates.[58]

Reaction to Plan

Senator Kennedy called Mr. Nixon's proposal for partnership with the insurance industry wasteful and inefficient and said that it would give the private insurance industry a windfall of billions of dollars annually.[59] Dr. Rashi Fein, Harvard medical economist, in an interview with the Washington *Post*, also saw the plan as a windfall for the insurance industry. "We will not be taking over a thriving industry," he said. "The reason the industry wants in is to make money. They haven't been making any money but they see a great potential."[60]

Einar Mohn, chairman of the California Council for Health Plan Alternatives, said the Nixon plan lacked quality and cost controls on hospitals and physicians. "The same old insurance industry would handle the program, and in the same old way," Mr. Mohn said.[61]

The administrator of New York City's health agency declared that the Nixon family health plan would provide less health care for the city's poor, rather than more. He pointed out that families earning from $3000 to $5000 would have to pay a significant sum for health costs that are now provided free under Medicaid in New York and some other states.[62]

The AFL-CIO executive council characterized the Nixon program as both piecemeal and inadequate. "It places main reliance on discredited private insurance, which has been largely responsible for the high cost, low quality medical care we have today," the council said.[63]

John G. Veneman, former California legislator and HEW Undersecretary for President Nixon, emphasized that the plan will require federal regulation of private insurers. Legislation authorizing transfer of state regulatory powers over private health insurance companies will be submitted to Congress, he said.[64]

Reaction of the American Medical Association was generally favorable to the Nixon plan.

NATIONAL PLAN SOON?

Under optimum circumstances national health insurance could provide most Americans with the quality medical services now enjoyed by a minority. It is important to realize, however, that merely providing a mechanism for paying health care bills does not guarantee availability or quality of service. Nor does it guarantee that services will be provided at a price that taxpayers or consumers can afford to pay.

The Medicare-Medicaid Experience

Government and consumer experience with Medicare and Medicaid underscores this statement. In the four years after Medicare went into effect, the price of medical services doubled while Medicaid costs quadrupled. In part these increases were due to inflation, yet medical care costs rose at twice the rate of increase in the general price level.

To facilitate passage of Medicare, Congress accepted many compromises calculated to obtain cooperation from the medical industry.[65] Professor Evaline M. Burns, social insurance expert, has pointed out that both Medicare and Medicaid started out on a pattern that interfered as little as possible with existing structural and administrative arrangements, methods of operation and remuneration, and professional mores and relationships.

> Hospitals will be paid their full reasonable costs for care given to the aged and indigent, doctors will be more sure of collecting full payment of their reasonable charges and left free to collect whatever unreasonable charges they can induce their aged patients to pay, and they can continue to insist on the fee-for-service principle. Insurance companies have been relieved of a burden and have been given a new claim on the loyalty of their customers in their capacity as helpful administrators of a large reimbursement program.[66]

Reimbursement Formulas

The legislation's reimbursement formulas, for hospitals on the basis of reasonable cost and for physicians on the basis of reasonable and customary fees, contributed heavily to the escalation of costs. The hospital formula provided no reward for efficient operation and made it easy for hospitals to pass on cost increases to third parties.

Reasonable fees for physicians are based on customary charges for similar services prevailing in the area, and thus should be no higher than those applicable for a comparable service, under comparable circumstances, to other policyholders and subscribers of the fiscal intermediary. Yet a report by staff members of the Senate Finance Committee in 1970 indicated that a great many doctors were billing Medicare more for the same services--in some cases up to four times more--than they charged such plans as Blue Shield.[67]

To combat this practice the committee staff recommended maximum fee schedules.[68] It called for an advisory board of actuaries and underwriters from private health insurance companies to assist in developing a schedule of allowances for surgical and medical services for each of the nine census regions in the country.*

Early in 1967, a report to the President emphasized that the Medicare reimbursement scheme tended to maintain institutions that are inefficient in size, plant layout and equipment.[69] The Social Security Amendments of 1967 therefore authorized the HEW secretary to experiment with alternative methods of reimbursement to provide incentives for limiting costs while maintaining or improving quality of care. The Senate Finance Committee in February 1970 again recommended creation of an incentive reimbursement system for doctors, hospitals and nursing homes to reward those who provide the same care less expensively.[70]

Fiscal Intermediaries

The Senate report also criticized the role of the insurance carriers authorized to act as fiscal intermediaries in the Medicare program.

> Carrier performance under Medicare has in the majority of instances been erratic, inefficient, costly

---

*Doctors who chose not to accept the fee schedule would bill and collect fees from patients directly, although the patient would be reimbursed only the amount on the schedule.

> and inconsistent with congressional intent. The Bureau of Health Insurance has taken little action to weed out and terminate the inefficient carrier. Extensive comparative data collected for the staff clearly indicate wide variation and frequent low levels of performance.[71]

Blue Cross (one fiscal intermediary) was blamed by a number of hospital administrators who testified before the Senate Health and Welfare Committee in January 1971. Three witnesses said that the relationship between Blue Cross and most of the nation's hospitals works to boost, not trim, patient bills. Hospitalization is encouraged even for routine tests, and hospitals often receive excessive reimbursement for services provided. "As this system now works, Blue Cross is reimbursing hospitals for whatever expenditures the hospital decides to make," one witness said.[72]

Blue Cross admitted it had not done all it could to hold down costs.[73] The Senate Antitrust and Monopoly Committee admitted that Blue Cross was guilty of some of the charges of inefficiency and waste made against it in earlier testimony.

Other Drawbacks

Besides the high-cost features, Medicare has other elements that militate against creation of a program that could provide quality medical care for the nation as a whole. Among these are commercial insurance practices that provide for reimbursement to the patient instead of the provider of services; absence of adequate controls over the fiscal intermediaries (discussed above); and use of deductibles and coinsurance that, together with the large number of noncovered services, greatly reduce the patient's financial protection.

The law's provision for deductibles and coinsurance represents a weakening of social insurance principles. It constitutes a barrier between the patient and services. In effect it divides the beneficiaries into two groups: (1) those who can afford to pay the deductible and coinsurance, who will receive benefits; and (2) those who cannot afford them and will be blocked off from benefits.

The procedures for obtaining benefits in a program where deductible and coinsurance apply throughout the entire range of covered services present real difficulties to the poorly educated as well as the aged patient. It is difficult for him to know what his rights are and how to claim them; he is required to keep records of expenditures, to fill out various claim forms, and to submit proofs of expenditures. It is questionable whether many claimants know what payments to make, when to make them, and to whom.

Testimony of leaders in the hospital and insurance professions before the House Ways and Means Committee indicated explicit disagreement with these provisions in Medicare. Walter J. McNerney, President of the Blue Cross Association, for example, testified that his organization believed that deductibles and coinsurance are undesirable in general hospital coverage, particularly for old people. He went on to say that if these provisions

> are small enough, they don't have any measurable effect on utilization. If they are large enough you run into danger of backfiring into underuse, which we all want to avoid.[74]

Kenneth Williamson, Associate Director of the American Hospital Association, opposed the provision because:

> We think that a deductible to serve a purpose--and that is

> erecting a barrier which is sufficient restraint against people being capricious in the use of hospitals--has to be pretty high. It has to have an impact. If you make it that high, then you hurt the people whom you most want to help, because they are the least able to afford the cost of the program.[75]

Cost of keeping account of the deductibles and coinsurance, moreover, could be so high that the system would gain little--except as the provision decreases utilization. Coinsurance may be useful to those whose first concern is to hold down costs or make a profit, but it does not help those whose first interest is the health of the population.

Testimony by Mr. McNerney at the hearings on the 1967 amendments indicated continued objection to the deductible provisions because of complex administration, excessive paperwork and cost, and confusion to aged beneficiaries.[76] Organized labor also testified against the provision in the belief that it caused financial hardship on the beneficiary and tended "to discourage early and continuous care and management of illness."[77] Melvin Glasser, director of the Social Security department of the United Automobile Workers, said:

> We have had now 20 years of experience in the UAW with prepaid medical care programs. There are no coinsurance and no deductibles in our basic medical care program for a reason.... We want to encourage early diagnosis and early treatment because that is good medical care, and we believe over the 20 years we have saved money, not lost, by not having coinsurance and deductibles.[78]

MULTIPLE SYSTEMS OF CARE

Impediments to providing efficient, economical, comprehensive health care for the nation are many. Institutional inertia and homo sapiens' resistance to change are not the least of them.* To adopt a national health care plan which would incorporate the shortcomings of Medicare would only compound past errors. Wilbur J. Cohen points out that providing insurance coverage for the millions now without it will increase demand. If the supply of personnel and facilities remains relatively limited over the short run and the free play of economic forces is allowed, prices may rise even more sharply than they have done in the past.

> It appears to me that the extension of voluntary health insurance or the enactment of federal legislation covering everyone in the nation under private or public insurance cannot be expected to stop or even significantly slow down increasing costs of medical care.[79]

Mr. Cohen holds that unless some reasonable solution to these problems is soon found, the inevitable consequence may be governmental operation and control of health services. That, he says, would be "socialized medicine."

In view of the current pressures for relief from burdensome medical costs, first steps toward an adequate national health care program cannot wait until all the ills of the medical industry are cured. Alternatives to adoption of a health insurance plan like Medicare should be considered, including a national health *service*, for example, that would provide direct medical service--a system Mr. Cohen calls socialized medicine.

---

*The writer assumes that financing such a system is not a basic problem in the richest country in the world. Only a reordering of priorities is necessary.

The federal government has had long experience with such a system in the armed services, in the Veterans' Administration and in the U.S. Public Health Service, as have the states with hospitals for mentally ill and for tuberculous persons. All these services are government organized, with salaried medical and other staff paid from general revenue funds. Although they are outside the free enterprise system, they are not considered socialistic.*

Direct services need not entail a huge federal bureaucracy. Providing health care service at the neighborhood level is a laudable concept that could be extended to persons with incomes above the poverty level.** A trend in this direction is the growing use throughout the country of community hospital emergency rooms--frequently called "drop-in clinics"--by persons demanding immediate attention in nonemergency situations. A neighborhood health center, which consolidates many ambulatory services under one roof and is sensitive to the needs of the surrounding population, is a form of health service delivery that has great potential, especially if it has community participation in its organization and governance. Medical staff in such centers would be salaried or paid on a capitation basis. Each center would be related to a community hospital. Financing would be through a Social Security "contribution" or through federal general revenue funds.

Development of these centers would fit into the philosophy embodied in the Kennedy bill as well as into

---

*Whether or not a government service is considered socialistic appears to depend on who gets it. Special tariffs, oil depletion allowances, cost-plus government contracts, "fair-trade" laws to provide a floor under prices, crop supports and agricultural subsidies have never been looked upon as socialistic.

**See p. 105 for description of neighborhood health centers for poverty groups.

the President's concept of health management organizations and might serve, temporarily, to remove the important problem of health care from the political arena.

Such a system would provide an effective alternative to the current anarchy of the medical industry or to a system of national health insurance which would allow that anarchy to continue. Such a system might further spur changes in the medical industry that would make comprehensive prepaid care available to everyone.

But quality medical services--preventive, curative and rehabilitative--provided wherever and whenever needed at a price the nation can afford cannot alone solve the nation's health problems. For medical services are useless without clean air, good nutrition, decent housing, meaningful employment and community acceptance of all its members, regardless of ethnic origin, religious or political views or lifestyle.

Notes

NOTES
to Preface

[1]Dorothy P. Rice and Barbara S. Cooper, "National Health Expenditures, 1929-70," *Social Security Bulletin*, 34(1): 3-18 (1971). See Table 5, p. 15.

[2]"Consumer Price Indexes, 1940-1970," *Social Security Bulletin*, 34(1): 63 (1971). See Table M-30. The consumer price index is a gauge of the cost of living for an average family.

[3]U.S. Department of Health, Education, and Welfare, Social Security Administration, Office of Research and Statistics, *National Health Expenditures, Fiscal Years 1929-1970*, by Barbara S. Cooper and Mary McGee (R & S Note No. 25) (Washington, D.C.: 1970), Table 5.

[4]Calculated from Health Insurance Institute, *1968 Source Book of Health Insurance Data* (New York: 1969), p. 31.

[5]California Department of Industrial Relations, Division of Labor Statistics and Research, "Health and Welfare Plans," *California Industrial Relations Reports*, No. 33 (1969), pp. 5-12.

[6]California Teachers Association, *District Paid Insurance Programs in California School Districts, 1968-1969* (Research Bulletin 232) (Burlingame, California: January 1969).

NOTES
to Chapter I

[1]See Rice and Cooper, Introduction, note 1 above.

[2]Loc. cit.

[3]Cooper and McGee, Table 9. See Introduction, note 3 above.

[4]Louis S. Reed, "Private Health Insurance, 1968," *Social Security Bulletin*, 32(12): 19-36 (1969), p. 31.

[5]For a full treatment of this subject, see J.F. Follmann, Jr., *Medical Care and Health Insurance* (Homewood, Illinois: Richard D. Irwin, Inc., 1963); and Herman M. and Anne R. Somers, *Doctors, Patients and Health Insurance* (Washington, D.C.: Brookings Institution, 1961).

[6]An interesting description of such benefits from the management view may be found in Benton H. Goodenough, "Health Care as a Fringe Benefit in Labor Contracts," *Public Health Reports*, 82(6): 513-518 (1967).

[7]Health Insurance Institute, *Health Insurance and Health Care Statistics* (New York: 1969), p. 9.

[8]Reed, Table 17, p. 33. See Ch. I, note 4 above.

[9]Robert D. Eilers and Robert M. Crowe, eds., *Group Insurance Handbook* (Homewood, Illinois: Richard D. Irwin, Inc., 1965), especially Part IV, pp. 229-372.

[10]California Department of Industrial Relations, Division of Labor Statistics and Research, "Prepaid Dental Care Plans," *California Industrial Relations Reports*, No. 33 (1969), pp. 13-68.

[11]Health Insurance Institute, p. 10. See Introduction, note 4 above.

[12]California Department of Industrial Relations, Division of Labor Statistics and Research, "Outpatient Prescription Drug Plans," *California Industrial Relations Reports*, No. 34 (1969), pp. 5-37.

[13]The Joint Information Service of the American Psychiatric Association and the National Association for Mental

Health, *Health Insurance for Mental Health*, by Patricia L. Scheidemandel, Charles K. Kanno and Raymond M. Glasscote (Washington, D.C.: 1968), p. 39.

[14]Ibid., p. 61.

[15]Ibid., pp. 32-33.

[16]Health Insurance Institute, p. 9. See Introduction, note 4 above.

NOTES
to Chapter II

[1]California Department of Industrial Relations, Division of Labor Statistics and Research, "Health and Welfare Plans," *California Industrial Relations Reports*, No. 33 (1969), pp. 5-12.

[2]U.S. Bureau of Labor Statistics, *Area Wage Survey, San Jose, California Metropolitan Area*, Bulletin 1660-24 (September 1969), Table B-6, p. 20; and *Area Wage Survey, San Francisco-Oakland Metropolitan Area*, Bulletin 1660-33 (October 1969), Table B-6, p. 34. The study excluded firms with fewer than 50 employees and in some cases firms with fewer than 100 employees.

NOTES
to Chapter III

[1]"Federal Employees Health Benefits," *Social Security Bulletin*, 33(11): 2 (1970).

[2]U.S. Civil Service Commission, Bureau of Retirement and Insurance, *Report*, fiscal year ended June 30, 1968 (Washington, D.C.: 1969), Tables C-3, C-5, pp. 33 and 35 respectively.

[3]California Public Employees Retirement System, *38th Annual Financial Report and Report of Operations for Fiscal Year Ended June 30, 1969* (Sacramento: 1970), p. 23.

[4]California Department of Finance, *California Administrative Code*, Title 2, Administration: Public Employees' Retirement System, Sec. 599.510.

[5]*California Government Code* Secs. 53201, 53202, 53205; *Education Code* Secs. 13009, 20806.

NOTES
to Chapter IV

[1]Rice and Cooper, Table 3, p. 10. See Introduction, note 1 above.

[2]Loc. cit.

[3]See Herman M. and Anne R. Somers, *Medicare and the Hospitals: Issues and Prospects* (Washington, D.C.: Brookings Institution, 1967), pp. 1-24. See also Margaret Greenfield, *Medicare and Medicaid, the 1965 and 1967 Social Security Amendments* (Berkeley: Institute of Governmental Studies, University of California, 1968), pp. 76-104.

[4]Rice and Cooper, note 1 above.

[5]Barbara S. Cooper, "Medical Care Outlays for Aged and Nonaged Persons, 1966-69," *Social Security Bulletin*, 33(7): 3-12 (1970), pp. 1, 10.

[6]U.S. Department of Health, Education, and Welfare, *Report of the Task Force on Medicaid and Related Programs* (Washington, D.C.: 1970). See also Greenfield, pp. 105-139, Ch. IV, note 3 above.

[7]Social Security Act, Title XIX, Sec. 1903(c)(4)(e) in 79 *Statutes at Large* (Stat.) 350.

[8]Rice and Cooper, p. 9. See Introduction, note 1 above.

[9]California Department of Social Welfare, *Public Welfare in California*, Statistical Series PA3-129 (June 1970). Figures based on Tables 3a and 3b.

[10]California Department of Health Care Services, *Notice of Emergency Action Taken on Regulations*, October 19, 1970.

[11]California Department of Health Care Services, *Recently Filed Medi-Cal Regulations*, July 24, 1970, Sec. 50607.

[12]For a description of earlier crises, see Margaret Greenfield, *Medi-Cal: The California Medicaid Program, 1966-1967* (Berkeley: Institute of Governmental Studies, University of California, 1970), pp. 53-60.

[13]California Department of Health Care Services, *Medi-Cal Letter No. 39-70 (CMAP)*, December 4, 1970.

[14]Problems entailed in supplying poverty populations with medical care are described in John C. Norman, ed., *Medicine in the Ghetto* (New York: Appleton-Century, Crofts, 1969). See also D.L. Madison, "Organized Health Care for the Poor," *Medical Care Review*, 26: 783-807 (1969).

[15]Office of Economic Opportunity, *The Neighborhood Health Center* (Washington, D.C.: 1968), p. 3. See also Count D. Gibson, Jr., "The Neighborhood Health Center: The Primary Unit of Health Care," *American Journal of Public Health*, 58(7): 1188-1191 (July 1968).

[16]L.B. Schorr and J.T. English, "Background, Context and Significant Issues in Neighborhood Health Center Programs," Milbank Memorial Fund *Quarterly*, 461: 289-296, Part 1 (1968).

[17]"Patients Will Have a Patio for Waiting," *California's Health*, 26: 8-9 (July 1968).

[18]"S.F. Mission Health Center the First Actively Backed by a Medical Society," *California's Health*, 25: 15-17 (November 1967).

[19]"Mission Neighborhood Health Center," *San Francisco Medical Society Bulletin* (July 1970), pp. 8-9.

[20]San Francisco *Chronicle*, February 24, 1970, p. 5.

NOTES
to Chapter V

[1]U.S. Department of Health, Education, and Welfare, Public Health Service, Health Services and Mental Health Administration, "Hospital and Surgical Insurance Coverage Among Persons Under 65 Years of Age in the United States, 1968 (Health Interview Survey from the National Center for Health Statistics)," *Monthly Vital Statistics Report*, 18: 1-4 (February 2, 1970); see also Charlotte Muller, "Income and the Receipt of Medical Care," *American Journal of Public Health*, 55(4): 510-521 (1965).

[2]New York *Times*, October 29, 1969, p. 22.

[3]Sacramento *Bee*, December 1, 1969, p. A3.

[4]U.S. Department of Health, Education, and Welfare, *A Report on the Health of the Nation's Health-Care System*, by Robert H. Finch and Roger O. Egeberg (Washington, D.C.: July 10, 1969).

[5]"Introduction of a Bill Establishing a Council of Health Advisers," *Congressional Record*, 115: S. 2898, September 16, 1969, Part 19, pp. 25539-25557; see also "U.S. Health Care Called Muddled in Senate Study," New York *Times*, March 17, 1970, p. 1.

[6]Walter J. McNerney, "The Health Administration Establishment: Underachiever," *American Journal of Public Health*, 59(10): 1799-1808 (1969).

[7]Herbert E. Klarman, "Increase in the Cost of Physician and Hospital Services," *Inquiry*, 7(1): 22-36ff. (1970).

[8]Herman M. and Anne R. Somers, pp. 197-198. See Ch. IV, note 3 above.

[9]*Task Force on Medicaid*, pp. 2, 106. See Ch. IV, note 6 above.

[10]San Francisco *Chronicle*, December 25, 1969, p. 6E.

[11]San Francisco *Chronicle*, October 30, 1970, p. 10.

[12]Carl M. Cobb, "Solving the Doctor Shortage," *Saturday Review*, 53: 24-26ff. (August 22, 1970). Other articles

in this issue also deal with problems in the delivery of medical care. See also "Medex," *Hospital Tribune*, 4: 1, 4 (September 21, 1970).

[13]California Medical Association, Bureau of Research and Planning, "Physician Assistants," *Socio-Economic Report*, 9(12): 1-5 (1969), esp. pp. 2-3. See also California Legislature, Assembly Interim Committee on Health and Welfare, *Physician's Assistant*, Transcript of Proceedings (December 4, 1969) (Sacramento: 1969).

[14]U.S. Congress, Senate Committee on Government Operations, Subcommittee on Executive Reorganization, *Health Care in America*, Hearings, 90th Cong. 2d Sess. (April 22-25, 1968) (Washington, D.C.: 1968), Part 1, p. 182.

[15]Ibid., p. 216. See also Mark V. Pauly, "Efficiency, Incentives and Reimbursement for Health Care," *Inquiry*, 7(1): 114-131 (1970).

[16]*Health Care in America*, p. 120. See Ch. V, note 14 above.

[17]See, for example, Mark H. Lepper, "Health Planning for the Urban Community: the Neighborhood Health Center," *Public Welfare*, 25(2): 141-149 (1967).

[18]U.S. Department of Health, Education, and Welfare, *Medical Care Prices*, A Report to the President (Washington, D.C.: February 1967), pp. 4-5.

[19]George S. Perrott and Jean C. Chase, "The Federal Employees Health Benefits Program, Fifth-Term Coverage and Hospital Utilization," *Group Health and Welfare News*, Special Supplement (May 1967), Figure I, p. vi.

[20]California Public Employees' Retirement System, Board of Administration, Medical Advisory Council, *Final Report on the Survey of Consumer Experience Under the State of California Employees' Hospital and Medical Care Act* (June 1968), p. 54.

[21]Ibid., p. 62.

[22]Richard E. Weinerman, "Patients' Perceptions of Group Medical Care, Review and Analysis of Studies on Choice and Utilization of Prepayment Group Practice

Plan," *American Journal of Public Health*, 54(6): 880-889 (1964).

[23]Richard M. Bailey, "Philosophy, Faith, Fact and Fiction in the Production of Medical Services," *Inquiry*, 7(1): 37-54 (1970).

[24]Harold F. Newman, "The Impact of Medicare on Group Practice Prepayment Plans," *American Journal of Public Health*, 59(4): 629-634 (1969), Table 1, p. 633.

[25]American Hospital Association and U.S. Public Health Service Joint Committee, *Areawide Planning for Hospitals and Related Health Facilities*, Public Health Service Publication No. 855 (July 1961), p. 1.

[26]U.S. Department of Health, Education, and Welfare, Secretary's Advisory Committee on Hospital Effectiveness, *Report* (Washington, D.C.: 1968), p. 12.

[27]Ibid., p. 13.

[28]Ibid., p. 27.

[29]U.S. Department of Health, Education, and Welfare, Social Security Administration, Office of Research and Statistics, "Improving the Effectiveness of Health Insurance and Prepayment" in *Private Health Insurance and Medical Care, Conference Papers* (Washington, D.C.: 1968), pp. 43-74. See esp. p. 50.

[30]Ibid., *Private Health Insurance...*, "Creating Competition in the Health-Care Industry," pp. 1-18.

[31]Ibid., pp. 7-8.

[32]Ibid., p. 12.

[33]Ibid., p. 14.

[34]See *Task Force on Medicaid*, pp. 71-74. Ch. IV, note 6 above. See also Herbert and Marilyn S. Notkin, "Community Participation in Health Services," *Medical Care Review*, 27(11): 1178-1201 (1970).

[35]Walter P. Reuther, "The Health Care Crisis: Where Do We Go From Here?" *American Journal of Public Health*, 59(1): 12-20 (1969), p. 15.

[36]San Francisco *Chronicle*, November 20, 1969, p. 6.

[37]Los Angeles *Times*, October 22, 1968, p. 3.

[38]California Council for Health Plan Alternatives, *Health and Welfare Report*, 3(1) (May 1970).

[39]New York *Times*, October 15, 1969, p. 24.

[40]U.S. Department of Health, Education, and Welfare, *Report of the National Conference on Medical Costs* (Washington, D.C.: June 27-28, 1967), p. 282.

[41]University of Chicago, Graduate School of Business, Center for Health Administration Studies, *National Health Insurance--Problems and Prospects*, by Wilbur J. Cohen (Chicago: 1970), pp. 11-12.

[42]Louis Harris, "The Harris Survey: Majority of U.S. Public Advocates Medicare for All, Not Just Elderly," Washington *Post*, January 23, 1967, p. A2.

[43]New York *Times*, September 2, 1969, p. 36 and September 3, 1969, p. 1.

[44]New York *Times*, February 23, 1967, p. 1.

[45]New York *Times*, September 19, 1969, p. 1.

[46]U.S. Interdepartmental Committee to Coordinate Health and Welfare Activities, *The Nation's Health*, Discussion at the National Health Conference, July 18-20, 1938 (Washington, D.C.: 1939), pp. 46-53.

[47]For more detailed descriptions of federal government and congressional interest, see Arthur J. Altmeyer, *The Formative Years of Social Security* (Madison: University of Wisconsin Press, 1966), esp. pp. 115-117, 146, 154, 171-173, 193-194, 252-255, 261-262. Also, U.S. Department of Health, Education, and Welfare, Social Security Administration, Office of Research and Statistics, *The Evaluation of Medicare*, by Peter A. Corning, Research Report No. 29 (Washington, D.C.: 1969).

[48]*Health Care in America*, Part 2, p. 744. See Ch. V, note 14 above.

[49]Ibid., p. 745.

[50]San Francisco *Chronicle*, September 25, 1970, p. 10.

[51]U.S. Department of Health, Education, and Welfare, Social Security Administration, Office of Research and Statistics, *National Health Insurance: A Comparison of Five Proposals*, by Saul Waldman and Evelyn Peel, R & S Note No. 12 (Washington, D.C.: 1970).

[52]San Francisco *Chronicle*, February 19, 1971, p. 1.

[53]New York *Times*, February 19, 1971, pp. 17-18.

[54]Loc. cit.

[55]Ibid., p. 16.

[56]Loc. cit.

[57]Loc. cit.

[58]Loc. cit.

[59]Ibid., p. 17.

[60]San Francisco *Chronicle*, February 23, 1971, p. 10.

[61]Loc. cit.

[62]New York *Times*, February 19, 1971, p. 9.

[63]San Francisco *Sunday Examiner & Chronicle*, February 28, 1971, "This World," p. 15.

[64]San Francisco *Chronicle*, February 20, 1971, p. 6.

[65]Somers and Somers, pp. 22-24. See Ch. IV, note 3 above.

[66]Eveline M. Burns, "Social Policy and the Health Services," *American Journal of Public Health*, 57(2): 199-212 (1967), p. 204.

[67]U.S. Congress, Senate Committee on Finance, *Medicare and Medicaid, Problems, Issues, and Alternatives, Report of the Staff* (February 9, 1970) (Washington, D.C.: 1970), pp. 60-67, 81-88.

[68]Ibid., pp. 67-69.

[69]*Medical Care Prices*, p. 8. See Ch. V, note 18 above.

[70]U.S. Congress, Senate Committee on Finance, *Report*, p. 89. See Ch. V, note 67 above.

[71]Ibid., pp. 20, 113-120. See Ch. V, note 67 above.

[72]San Francisco *Chronicle*, January 28, 1971, p. 7.

[73]San Francisco *Chronicle*, January 29, 1971, p. 10.

[74]U.S. Congress, House Committee on Ways and Means, *Medical Care for the Aged*, Executive Hearings, 89th Cong., 1st Sess. (January 27-28, February 1-10, 16, 1965) (Washington, D.C.: 1965), Part 1, p. 168.

[75]Ibid., p. 289.

[76]U.S. Congress, Senate Committee on Finance, *Social Security Amendments of 1967, Hearings* (August 28-31, September 11, 12, 18, 19, 1967) (Washington, D.C.: 1967), Part 2, pp. 920-922.

[77]Ibid., Part 3, p. 1682.

[78]Ibid., p. 1654; see also Shirley Jesmer and Robert J. Scharfenberg, "Problems in Measuring the Effect of Deductibles Upon Hospital Utilization," *Blue Cross Reports*, 6(5): 1-7 (October 1968).

[79]Wilbur J. Cohen, pp. 20-21. See Ch. V, note 41 above.

Appendix

(SAMPLE QUESTIONNAIRE)

No._____

University of California
Institute of Governmental Studies
Berkeley, California 94720

HEALTH INSURANCE IN THE SAN FRANCISCO BAY AREA

1. How many residents of Bay Area counties does your firm employ? _____

   (Bay Area counties: Alameda, Contra Costa, Marin, Napa, San Francisco, San Mateo, Santa Clara, Solano, Sonoma)

2. Does your firm offer employees a basic medical and surgical insurance program? Yes ( ) No ( )

   NOTE: If you have checked "no" to question 2, the rest of this schedule is not pertinent. We would appreciate your returning it to us without delay. Thank you.

* * *

3. If your reply to question 2 is "yes," please check whether the program originated in a collective bargaining agreement. Yes ( ) No ( )

4. Please state the number of persons in each classification who participate in the program.

Classification	Employees	Dependents	Retired
Salaried	_____	_____	_____
Hourly	_____	_____	_____
Other (specify)	_____	_____	_____

5. Please state what proportion of premium costs the firm pays for each classification.

Classification	Employees	Dependents	Retired
Salaried	_____%	_____%	_____%
Hourly	_____%	_____%	_____%
Other	_____%	_____%	_____%

6. Please state whether your program offers employees alternative health insurance plans. Yes ( ) No ( )

7. Please check whether the plans offered are underwritten by:

Insurance companies	_____
Medical society foundation	_____
Blue Shield-Blue Cross	_____
Prepaid comprehensive group practice	_____
Other (specify) ____________________	_____

8. Please check whether employees may also choose group major medical coverage. Yes ( ) No ( )

9. If major medical coverage is available, please indicate:

How many employees are covered	_____
What proportion of the premium the firm pays	_____%

* * *

NOTE: The questions below are designed to ascertain the principal benefits of company health insurance plans. If your company has more than one plan, answers to the following questions should be applied to the basic plan covering the greatest number of employees.

10. Please check the type of plan to which the answers below apply.

Insurance companies	____
Medical society foundation	____
Blue Shield-Blue Cross	____
Prepaid comprehensive group practice	____
Other (specify) ________________	____

11. Please indicate below the specific benefits provided and the maximum limitation on each. If there is no maximum, please enter "0."

Hospitalization

Room and board:	Maximum amount per day	$____
	Maximum number of days	____
	per illness	____
	per year	____
Other charges:	Maximum limitation	$____
Surgical Benefits	Maximum limitation	$____

Physician Visits

Hospital:	Max. fee $____	Max. no. visits ____
Office:	Max. fee $____	Max. no. visits ____
Home:	Max. fee $____	Max. no. visits ____

12. Do benefits include psychiatric care?
Yes ( ) No ( )

13. If yes, please check if benefit covers treatment:

In hospital	____
In clinic	____
In physician's office	____

14. Please check whether benefits for psychiatric illness are:

    Same as for physical illness _____
    More limited than for physical illness _____

15. Please check whether insurance plan also covers:

    Dental care _____
    Eye care _____
    Prescription drugs _____

16. Please check whether benefits for dependents are:

    Same as those for the primary policyholder _____
    Less than those for the primary policyholder _____

____
Name of person replying

____
Title

THANK YOU FOR YOUR PATIENCE AND COOPERATION!